The DNA of Leadership

To your great leadership!

Myron

The DNA of Leadership

Creating Healthy Leaders and Vibrant Organizations

Myron Beard and Alan Weiss

BUSINESS EXPERT PRESS

The DNA of Leadership: Creating Healthy Leaders and Vibrant Organizations

First published in 2017 by
Business Expert Press, LLC
222 East 46th Street, New York, NY 10017
www.businessexpertpress.com

ISBN-13: 978-1-63157-789-5 (paperback)
ISBN-13: 978-1-63157-790-1 (e-book)

Business Expert Press Human Resource Management and Organizational Behavior Collection

Collection ISSN: 1946-5637 (print)
Collection ISSN: 1946-5645 (electronic)

Cover and interior design by Exeter Premedia Services Private Ltd., Chennai, India

First edition: 2017

10 9 8 7 6 5 4 3 2 1

Printed in the United States of America.

Abstract

The DNA of Leadership: Creating Healthy Leaders and Vibrant Organizations

Much like DNA provides the structure and design for life, the DNA of leadership defines the essential characteristics required to become an outstanding leader. This book is the result of working with thousands of executives, reviewing their behaviors, and identifying what is required for high levels of success. The authors' expertise encompasses the nexus of psychology and executive coaching, and they have identified several essential characteristics, including:

- Setting a forceful vision
- Identifying and hiring extraordinary talent
- Delegating for leveraging of results
- Communicating for impact
- Having difficult conversations
- Creating a compelling business model

You will learn powerful and practical approaches to *change* your behavior, in order to become a truly outstanding leader. Each chapter has a **Coach's Corner** that crystallizes the lessons of the chapter, while challenging leaders to identify *key behaviors* they need to modify to become truly outstanding. The interactive last chapter provides specific tools to help leaders take control of their future by creating specific **Personal Goal Plans** toward their most compelling goals. The DNA of Leadership is not just a book. It is an active roadmap for moving a leader toward greatness. This book is for leaders at every level in an organization from the first-time manager to the chief executive officer (CEO). There are ideas for everyone here.

Keywords

accountability, business model, communication, conflict, delegation, development, executive, executive development, goal setting, goals, high-performing teams, hiring, leader, leadership development, leadership, management, management development, managing millennials, millennials, onboarding, problem-solving, self-confidence, strategic thinking, strategy, team, teamwork, vision, visionary

Contents

Acknowledgments

The writing of a book involves many people. First, I am immensely indebted to my coauthor, Alan Weiss. I am grateful that he has been both a mentor and a close ally in the writing and publishing of our book. It is safe to say that, without Alan's support and encouragement, this book would not have been written! The advice and counsel he has provided have been priceless. Also, I appreciate Rob Zwettler at Business Expert Press for his guidance and encouragement in completing the book. Special thanks go to Noelle Livengood, who provided assistance with the graphics and the captions and added greater interest and humor to each chapter.

My personal thanks go to a team of my family members whose help was invaluable. First, my dear wife, Ann Beard, gave countless hours in editing and making the work understandable and easier to read. My youngest son, Matthew Beard, asked provocative questions and added great creativity that made each chapter come to life. My oldest son, Andrew Beard, read the manuscript with fresh eyes and could see where changes needed to be made. I am grateful to each of you for your considerable and important contributions to the book and to my life. Last, but not least, I am thankful for the many leaders from whom I have learned so much about business and leadership.

—Myron Beard

I would like to thank the hundreds of thousands of people around the world who have worked with me personally, attended my events, watched my videos, listened to my podcasts, read my newsletters, and purchased my books. I always learn more than anyone else, and I am indebted to all of you for your continuing support. My thanks also to my coauthor, Myron Beard, who conceived of and invited me to participate in this project.

—Alan Weiss

Introduction and Overview

In *The DNA of Leadership: Creating Healthy Leaders and Vibrant Organizations*, we are presenting our observations of leadership from working side-by-side with leaders for over 50 years combined. From our work, we have come to understand which qualities and practices are the necessary foundations for successful executives and leaders. By evaluating and interviewing thousands of executives, we have identified key leadership characteristics that are *essential* for leadership success. These are not merely superficial characteristics possessed only by great leaders, but rather, they are the building blocks that make a leader truly great. We call them the DNA of leadership. When done well, these skills can vault a leader to new levels of success.

Our interest in creating this book is to give our readers the same kind of development experience as the leaders with whom we have worked. We want to give good leaders the tools they need to become great leaders through actual *behavioral change*. Changing behavior is more than having the right information. In this book, we stress carefully selecting a limited number of goals on which to focus and using the tools we present to facilitate accomplishing those goals.

Each chapter includes a **Case Study** that provides a real-life illustration of the theme of the chapter. At the end of each chapter, we have our **Coach's Corner,** where we turn experiences and lessons from our clients into practical ideas, suggestions, and exercises. The work on your chosen developmental goals comes together in our last chapter, in which we present a complete guide for turning goals into actions, the **Personal Goal Plan**.

It is our hope that, like many of the leaders with whom we have worked, you will be able to identify those changes that would make the most important difference for you and your company. Much like a small change in a person's genetic code can have a great impact on his or her life, we believe that a small change in the DNA of leadership can lead to huge results. We hope to contribute to your becoming a great leader and invite you to read on.

CHAPTER 1

Leadership Implosion: Failure to Change = Failure to Thrive

Jonathan Schwartz was promoted internally to chief executive officer (CEO) of Sun Microsystems in 2006 after serving in a number of vice presidential roles. Under Schwartz's direction, the company hemorrhaged its value and was eventually sold to Oracle in 2010 and subsequently dismantled. Similarly, Marissa Mayer was brought on as CEO of Yahoo in 2012 after a successful tenure at Google, where she served as the company's first female engineer and moved on to several senior roles. Mayer was brought in from outside the company and failed to make a successful transition to CEO at Yahoo, never implementing a cohesive strategy. She has been criticized for relying on business practices that had served her well at her former position but turned out to be ineffective at Yahoo. In both of these cases, there are indications that the failing executives demonstrated an extreme lack of understanding and appreciation for the scope and scale of their new positions.

When executives fail to meet the expectations of their roles, it is typically not a matter of intelligence, drive, energy, persistence, or intent. According to the Corporate Executive Board, 50 to 70 percent of executives fail within the first 18 months of promotion into an executive role. About 3 percent "fail spectacularly" while about 50 percent "quietly struggle."[1] This failure rate might be better understood in the case of an outside hire who is unfamiliar with the business and lacks knowledge of the culture. However, this failure rate remains true whether or not the new leader has been promoted from within or from outside the company! It is more perplexing how an internal promotion of someone would fail since they are familiar with the people, products, and customers. The fact that so many internal and external executives fail not only hurts a company, but also has long-term implications for succession planning and business continuity. In our mapping of the DNA of leadership, we have identified several common causes for these types of leadership failures.

Moving Up: Rocky Ride or Smooth Transition

In corporate America, the prevailing notion is that if you work hard and do quality work, success and recognition will follow. Very little attention is given to *the perils of advancement*. In fact, the higher up one moves in any organization, the more important it is to do things *fundamentally differently* and to adopt a significantly different leadership paradigm. This change requires moving well out of your comfort zone and trusting that, by adopting new behaviors, you can continue to be successful at this new level. Individuals frequently move up in organizations because of their ability to get tactical work completed. They become successful at the deep and narrow tasks without having developed a broader, longer-term view of the business. They assume that they will be successful in their new role by doing more of the same. In our experience, one of the great leadership failures is the inability of leaders to move into more strategic-thinking roles and out of their previously primarily tactical roles.

John Kotter, Harvard Business School professor, has noted that management is about coping with complexity, whereas leadership is about dealing with change. Becoming adept at short-term tactical execution is necessary for moving into higher levels in an organization. However, staying in a tactical mode will not ultimately advance a career. There are two dimensions of focus in leadership—the tactical/operational and the strategic dimensions. These dimensions are typically, though not always, linked to time. Tactical activities are usually more of short term in nature while strategic activities are usually of longer term.

Figure 1.1 demonstrates these differences and provides the *pathway* for moving from operational tacticians to strategic leaders. In the *lower left quadrant*, you will note the short-term, present-time, tactical, and operational issues. These tasks and initiatives must be executed just to keep the doors of a business open. This is the "engine" of a business. If the operations of a business are not functioning well, strategy is useless. However,

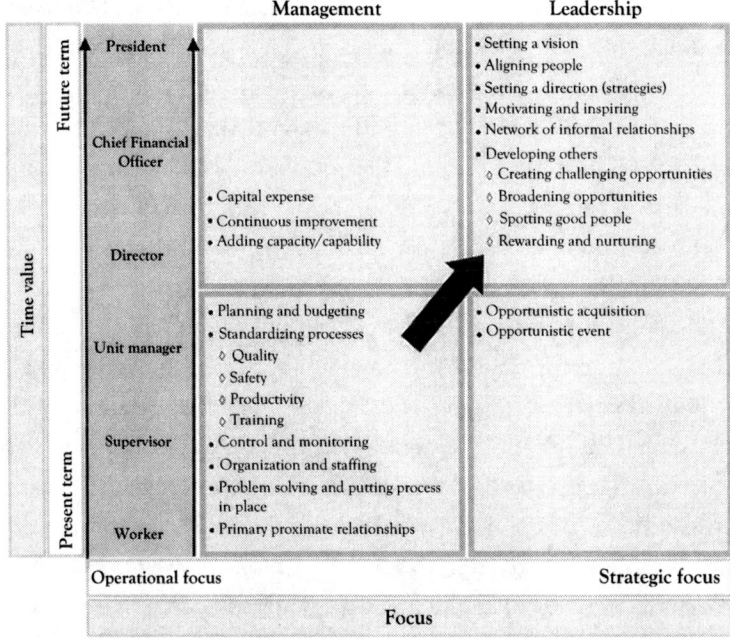

Figure 1.1 Migrating to Leadership

well-functioning operations without strategy are a recipe for stagnation and eventual decline. The leader must ensure continuity of efficient operations while, also, looking out for the future of the organization.

The *upper right quadrant* represents the longer-term, strategic focus a leader must embrace and drive in order to help the business sustain success in the future. Note how different the foci of the two quadrants are. Strategic issues are all about longer-term succession planning; new markets; what customers will want in the future; possible acquisition targets; industry, governmental, and regulatory relationships; and setting a vision for the organization. Early in his tenure at GE, Jack Welch focused on drastically cutting costs to salvage the business. He eliminated 135,000 jobs in streamlining the business. He knew that the engine of the business was broken and needed repair. He was not afraid to "dip down" into the operations of the business to fix it. However, over time, he had the wisdom to recognize that, strategically, it is *people* who are at the heart of continuing to grow a business. Under his direction, he transformed the GE Management Development Institute, referred to as Crotonville, to build a new breed of leaders for GE. Ultimately, Crotonville offered over 1,800 courses to GE management throughout the world. Welch taught monthly at Crotonville and put into practice what he preached. As a result of his focus on developing leaders, when Welch left GE, the GE Board of Directors had several excellent internal candidates to consider for his position before selecting Jeff Immelt. This is a supreme example of a leader focusing on the strategic, long-term vision of a company.

It is always better when a leader understands the culture of a business and is able to incorporate that understanding into his or her thinking. The leader must have a degree of confidence that the operations of the business are running effectively and efficiently. He or she must also have ensured that the appropriate resources are available to run the operations. It is only then that the leader can begin to change his or her attention to the organization's strategy. This is the art of *managing the intersection* between the operational and the strategic. He knows when it is advantageous to get involved in operations and when it is advantageous to take a broader view. The successful executive develops a sense of both timing and degree of attention required of both.

Welch captured this *managing-the-intersection* challenge by saying, "You can't grow long-term if you can't eat short-term. Anybody can manage short. Anybody can manage long. Balancing those two things is what management is." As hockey great Wayne Gretzky has said, "a good player skates to where the puck is. A great player skates to where the puck will be." A great leader *anticipates* where the business will be and begins making adaptations and revisions to get there. This anticipation requires more time spent in study, reflection, and utilization of the broader overall perspective of leadership, instead of viewing in depth the various parts of the organization.

Reestablishing Priorities: Identifying What Matters Now

You may be asking yourself where, and how, should the leader focus his or her attention? Imagine it is your first day on your new job. You have just been promoted and have moved into your big, new corner office. It is much nicer than you have had in the past, spacious with windows and a nice view, a mahogany desk and shelving, a small conference table, a wallboard with pens and an eraser. You have done well. After you settle in, you meet with your new executive assistant to review the pressing items you need to attend. After some brief chit-chat, you ask what she has noted for you. She informs you that you have several important issues *today*, including:

- The president is having a meeting that she wants you to attend.
- You have received 43 e-mails you need to answer.
- You need to discuss an employee crisis with human resources (HR).
- Legal wants to talk to you about a contract issue.
- The quality person wants to discuss product defects.
- An unhappy customer has serious quality concerns.
- Four other groups want you to be involved in meetings about initiatives for your advice and counsel.
- You have 12 voice mails from well-wishers, operations, marketing, and customers.
- Your husband has called to remind you that your daughter's ballet performance is later today.
- Your new team would like to take you out to lunch to congratulate you.
- You have a staff meeting in the afternoon.

Figure 1.2 Managing priorities

Source: Indomercy2012/Depositphotos. com. http://depositphotos.com/73524899/stock-illustration-businessman-doing-multitask-work. html (accessed October 26, 2016).

Your executive assistant also mentions that 7 to 15 additional requests have come in while you were meeting. Welcome to the big leagues!!!

The new leader will find that the demands of the executive position increase *exponentially*. Because it is a higher-profile position, the leader will have visibility from others in the organization that did not exist prior to the promotion. Others in the company will see the leader as an influential resource and request to include him or her in all sorts of initiatives, committees, and meetings. In responding alone, the sheer number of requests can drain valuable time from a leader and dilute his or her impact.

Illustration: What do you see in the picture to the right?

_____

_____

Most people viewing this picture indicate that they see a box with a dot in the middle. What they overlook is the fact that 99 percent of the picture is *whitespace*. It is sometimes in the whitespace that the most important things happen. One of the leader's main objectives is to identify what to focus on and what to ignore. The amount of data and information presented to a leader regularly can be overwhelming. The leader needs to focus attention on detecting the important priorities that matter in driving the business forward, not simply improving what is already in place. Improving and maintaining what is already in place is the responsibility of managers not the leader!

This act of filtering is the essence of all data analysis techniques. It is the foundation for the leader's identification of important data and information. All predictions should be made based on the most important data. New leaders often make the mistake of focusing on the most obvious, ostensibly urgent, issues (the dot in the middle of the square) instead of keeping a laser focus on the ones that are the most important for plotting the future (the whitespace). These urgent issues could often be handled by others, freeing up the leader's time for the important tasks. Leaders need to focus on those issues and data that will make a difference long term, not those that pull them back into the ongoing operations of the business. The ability to *differentiate* between those issues that genuinely require the leader's attention and those that should be delegated or ignored is, in effect, *managing the whitespace.*

In managing the whitespace, the leader must resist the urge to simply do *more of the same* and begin to do things *essentially differently*. In fact, what differentiates the leader from being another good employee is the

Case Study
From Pipefitter to Leader

A major construction company wanted to open a regional office in a new geographic area that showed promise. They appointed a general manager (GM) who had been successful in the field. He began in the company as a pipefitter, moved up to be a project engineer and then to a supervisor overseeing the construction of large projects. After a year in his new position, the GM was struggling to achieve the success expected. We were hired to help the company understand the obstacles preventing the GM from succeeding.

After numerous interviews, themes emerged including the fact that the GM spent too much time at construction sites rolling up his sleeves to work beside laborers and he did not spend enough time developing the business. He was neglecting to network with key customers and significant business and governmental influencers. When these issues were presented to the new GM, he acknowledged that he had difficulty changing his thinking from a cost-conscious project manager to an executive comfortable spending the money required to free his time to develop the business strategically. In addition, he saw the success of projects as his responsibility and had difficulty delegating work to others. When the urgency of changing his approach was presented to him, he began hiring and promoting individuals to oversee the construction so that he could begin engaging in the important strategic networking critical for success. While thinking and behaving strategically were foreign to him, he realized that he had to do change. Within three months of receiving this feedback, both the manager and home office began to see a significant turnaround in the business. Within a year the business had taken off.

leader's ability to identify, adopt, and drive change throughout the organization. The focus of operations, as illustrated in Figure 1.1, is to have a short-term tactical focus where processes are followed, outcomes are consistent, and day-to-day work is predictable. The leader's focus needs to be changing the organization to meet future challenges and opportunities, rather than simply making the company better able to address today's market needs. The new leader's focus should include looking at new markets or product offerings; identifying better, more effective distribution channels (e.g., Amazon); getting a perspective of the business from the inside-out (e.g., from the customer); overseeing talent management; and exploring how technology can fundamentally change the business (e.g., Netflix).

In our aforementioned example, the new, overwhelmed leader must focus on several things immediately, often, and consistently to survive and thrive. Here are some keys to help focus on the important over the familiar or lower level tasks.

- Understand clearly your manager's expectations of your role. This is the person you definitely need to please.
- Identify the top 2 to 3 objectives that you need to accomplish during the course of the year.
- Use these objectives as criteria for all the work you take on, triaging the work into:
  1. Only I can do it.
  2. This work can be delegated.
  3. This is not worthy of my time and can be eliminated.

You must be ruthless in deciding what you will, and will not, take on. Otherwise you are on a slow path downward and, probably, out of your job! Jonathan Schwartz, from our aforementioned example, was criticized for putting his focus into interfacing with customers through his blog rather than putting his focus into strategy. His CEO blog sought to, "drive awareness for the company, its products and ideas." Instead, it served more as a distraction. This is a case of him being so focused on the dot that the whitespace totally evaded him, causing him to overlook the essential strategy for the survival of the company.

Changing Focus: Trading the Microscope for the Telescope

Watching the interaction between a NASCAR driver and his or her pit mechanics in a professional auto race is a thing of joy. To watch the driver pull into the pit and the pit crew quickly and efficiently change tires, fuel the vehicle, or work on mechanical problems, is an amazing sight to behold. It is a wonderful example of the results of putting the right people in the right place and training them to follow clear, standardized processes very carefully.

The casual observer would believe that the crew and driver are the keys to the success of the race. However, what they would probably miss is the most important person in the race—the spotter.

Figure 1.3 Working in the Pit

Source: Pitstop-Leks/Depositphotos.com. http:// depositphotos.com/11441581/stock-illustration-pit-stop.html (accessed October 26, 2016).

The spotter is the member of the team who has an elevated position up in the grandstand and is the one guiding the driver in the race. The spotter is responsible for identifying and communicating the risks and opportunities for the driver. These would include changing track and weather conditions, studying crashes and places to exercise caution, identifying upcoming opportunities to take more risk, and knowing how and where to maneuver around other cars. The spotter becomes the "eyes" of the driver and is able to see farther ahead in order to identify ways for the driver to be more successful. The pit crew performs critical tactical tasks through highly standardized procedures, in a consistent manner that is seamless to the driver. The driver makes hundreds of tactical, moment-by-moment decisions based both on personal experience and on the input from the spotter. The spotter is the one identifying opportunities and risks and giving the strategic counsel for the driver's tactical decision-making.

This is a good metaphor for the work of the strategic leader. Moving up in an organization means, that to be successful, you increasingly have to identify a broader picture of both near-term and long-term risks and opportunities. This has been referred to as *working on* the business, not *in* the business. The individuals *working in* the business are responsible for getting products to the customer with careful consideration given to timeliness, cost, and quality. *Working in* the business is a tactical affair necessary for keeping the business going through well-developed operational processes to build quality products inexpensively, manage inventory, and oversee distribution channels to get products to customers on time. *Working on* the business requires a different mind-set. Moving from tactical day-to-day operations in the pit to a more strategic position in the grandstand requires making a big change in how you view the whole business. While the newly appointed leader will always be invested in what is going on at all levels, the focus of the leader needs to be on areas such as looking for new markets, innovation, establishing relationships with potential new customers, succession planning, and industry-wide leadership. These areas are all related to the leader's responsibility for giving future business direction.

Often, new leaders are tempted to get back down into "the pit" because it is their comfort zone and becomes their default. In addition, they typically do not get much, if any, direction on what it means to think more strategically or to grow the business. The difficulty of changing from being a tactical doer to a strategic thinker and future-oriented planner gets lost in the excitement of the move. While everyone wants the big corner office, it is not easy to change your thinking. New leaders need to adopt a completely new business paradigm "from the grandstand."

The Success Paradox: Growing More by Doing Less

Perfectionism is the enemy of the good. The need for a leader to maintain total control in a rapidly growing business is ultimately a self-defeating proposition. Moving into leadership means *giving up some control* and learning to trust so that the leader can leverage his or her skills through others. Early in a business, there *is* a need for the individual's control of business services or products, the people, and the process until the company reaches a point of critical mass of business or revenue. However, once this point has been reached, it is the leader's *inability to relinquish the right amount of control* to his or her employees that threatens to limit the business from growing and flourishing.

You can see in Figure 1.4 the point at which the behavior of a leader must change in order to continue to create sustainable growth. Both companies in the chart have an initial period of growth during which their founder *must control* most of the aspects of the business. In Company B, the business reaches a critical mass of work or revenue and an *inflection*

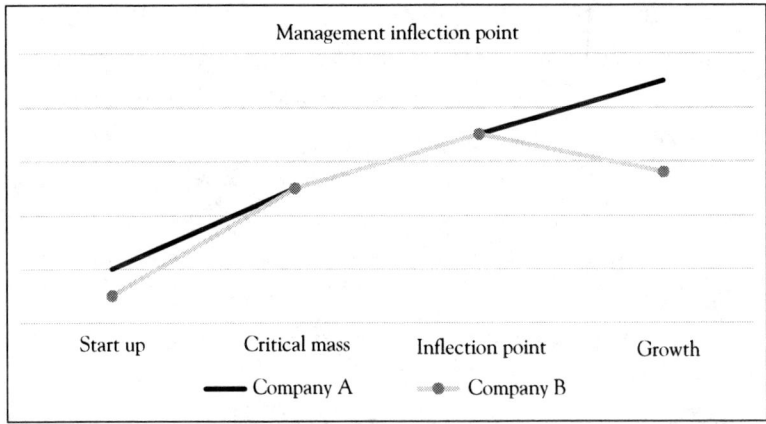

Figure 1.4 Management inflection point

point is reached when the leader needs to decide whether to adjust his or her management style or not. This founder has decided to continue to maintain control. As work begins to overwhelm the leader, growth stalls and may even begin to diminish as customers leave due to quality or timeliness issues.

In Company A, the same critical mass of business is achieved but, at the inflection point, this leader chose to relinquish some control, and delegate and empower employees to *work in* the business while he or she *worked on* the business. The potential for future growth becomes exponentially greater than that in Company B.

The fallacy of trying to control all of the major aspects of the business, after it has grown to a certain size, is that the ability to leverage other employees is lost. When the owner is either doing all of the business functions, or *micromanaging* those to whom

Figure 1.5 Micromanaging

Source: andrewgenn/Depositphotos.com. http://deposit-photos.com/75648217/stock-photo-micro-praise.html (accessed April 1, 2017).

he or she has assigned duties, a gridlock ensues. In a growing business, there is increasingly more activity than one person can manage—sales, financials, manufacturing, quality control, inventory control, order fulfillment, and distribution. As business activity mounts, the leader must undergo a significant management shift that requires relinquishing some control, delegating and empowering employees to do their jobs without micromanaging. Once the business has reached this critical mass, the manager must shift attention to strategic issues that will ensure the viability of the business in the future. This requires delegating and empowering.

This does not mean that the leader completely walks away from the tactical side of the business. It means that the relationship with the workings of the business move from doing work to monitoring the outcomes of work. For example, creating dashboards to monitor cost, productivity, on-time delivery, breakage, quality control, and inventory can become one way the leader oversees the business. The leader can always dip back into the business if there are temporary problems, but he or she can no longer *stay* involved in every detail. The leader, like the spotter, needs to raise his or her sights to grow the business, identify new customers, look for trends and innovations, and develop strategic relationships. Both the inside and outside of the business are important. One person simply cannot manage both sides at the same time.

Engaging Colleagues: Changing the Relationship Dynamic

While internal promotions send a positive message within a company about the opportunity for employees to move up, there are also unintended consequences associated with these promotions. In a matter of a single day, an internal promotion elevates an individual to being manager of those who were peers or friends previously. When people with whom you have worked side-by-side suddenly become your subordinates, the relationship dynamics change instantly. Problems around boundaries, reshuffling the deck, and managing "friends" can create a number of issues that can undermine the effectiveness of a new leader. Make no mistake, there are very likely to be repercussions from those with whom the promoted leader were previously peers. As Gore Vidal said, "any time a friend succeeds, I die a little." Internal promotions are always a time for personal reflection and reassessment when a colleague becomes the manager.

External responses to the promoted leader are typically congratulatory. However, privately, previous peers who have not been promoted often have feelings ranging from anger and resentment (why him or her and not me?); to disbelief (are you kidding me?). The degree to which the new manager actively sought the new position also affects the feelings and behaviors of others. The more obviously the leader has sought the new position, the more heightened the responses of previous peers will be. Regardless of the situation, there will be the unintended consequences of feelings and behavior from those "left behind."

In addition to taking on the responsibilities of a new position, the newly promoted leader will have to deal with the politics of managing former peers. What is the best way to deal with this situation? There are some very important points the new leader needs to address early on in his or her tenure.

- **Acknowledgment**: Publicly acknowledge the awkwardness of the situation—being peer one day and the leader the next. This needs to be done *unapologetically* and with a recognition that, in order to be successful, the support of the subordinate team will be essential. This should not take place with any false humility but with a recognition that they have been, in part, already responsible for the success of their new leader.
- **Leveraging Subordinate Skills**: Point out to the group that no one knows their skills and abilities better than "one of their own." This is a huge advantage in that the right skill set will continue to be, or begin to be, aligned with the right positions. This not only has the potential of accelerating the development of people, but it will also maintain or increase productivity.
- **Focus on the Goals**: Ultimately, it is the goals of the organization that should drive all behaviors. The importance of reiterating the goals that the team is expected to accomplish should be the single-most unifying factor. The

accomplishment of organizational goals is good for everyone and has the potential impact of providing new opportunities for all on the team.

- **Reset Boundaries**: Recalibrating boundaries is the most difficult and awkward item for the new leader to undertake. Transitioning to being the leader from having been a peer, colleague, and, in some instances, a social friend is critical to being successful. If boundaries are not reset, and behaviors changed, the leader runs the risk of appearing to play favorites. Having private conversations with social friends to reset these boundaries is uncomfortable, but necessary. For the most part, the leader should only socialize with subordinates as a group (e.g., team building) or on a rotating basis (e.g., having lunch with each person on a rotating basis).

- **Running the Business**: The quickest way to create the "new normal" is for the new leader to take charge of the business and exercise clear authority on a day-to-day basis. People deal much better with certainty and routine than with not knowing what to expect. The sooner a clear routine is established, the sooner productivity returns and destructive political behavior is curtailed.

A second, but equally important, issue to address is the relationships with new peers—those who were previously superior to the new leader. Moving from taking direction from a superior to sitting at the same table as an equal is a major shift in a relationship. While the drama and politics of becoming a new peer are not usually as profound, there can be an awkward "onboarding" period. As with previous peers, everyone will typically be on his or her best behavior and be congratulatory. However, behind the public laudatory comments, there is also the possibility of some psychological disruption occurring. At this level, there is often scrutiny to determine if the new leader is really deserving to be "one of us." With few exceptions, the competitiveness of others will kick in and they may feel threatened by the new addition to their management team.

Many questions about the new leader will surface—either overtly or covertly. Questions include: Does the new leader have the capabilities, both intellectually and personally, that are commensurate with others at this level? How will the new leader fit into the existing team of peers? Will the new leader be a team player? Can he or she be trusted? What approach should the new leader take to address the concerns of his or her new peers? In initial interactions with the new peer group, consider the following:

- **Approach**: In a grateful but confident manner express how pleased you are to be part of the new peer group. Keep in mind that the promotion was not because of luck, but because you earned it. Acknowledge the satisfaction of being part of this group without being obsequious or deferential.
- **Meetings**: Schedule a one-on-one meeting with each of your new peers to get to know them, and learn how and why you and your group can support/work with them. Understand their unique skills and share yours with them.
- **Synergy**: Identify ways you can help your new peers be more successful. In a tangible and meaningful way, identify mutually beneficial opportunities to work synergistically with them.

The new leader would be wise to recognize the unintended and complex relational issues associated with the promotion and address them early, unapologetically and directly. Now that the new leader is thinking at the right level and has resolved major relationship issues, what is the next area of attention?

Coach's Corner

Leaders are paid to make a difference. The degree, and speed, with which they adapt to their positions determines how quickly the changes required for continued business achievements can be made. Leaders must simultaneously "shake the dust off of their shoes" and adopt a new, more strategic way of looking at the business. Below are the areas that leaders must master in order to become effective and successful in their positions.

Four Tips for Avoiding Leadership Implosion

1. **Migrating to Leadership**
   - Being a good manager means dealing with day-to-day specifics and putting out fires. Being a good leader means expanding your vision and seeing what is best for your organization's future.

2. **Changing Your Vision**
   - As you move up in an organization your workflow must pivot from direct operations management to strategic planning. At the top levels of an organization, you must go from working *in* the business to working *on* the business.

3. **Changing Your Focus**
   - The higher you rise in an organization, the more disparate tasks will be thrust at you. The best leaders know where to place focus and how to delegate or scrap what is not of core importance.

4. **Making the Relational Leap**
   - After being promoted do not neglect managing relationships with former peers and new colleagues. Be proactive in realigning and defining your newly altered relationships.

Areas for Development

Now, from the aforementioned assessment, list any items in which you scored in the *"Much too Little"* or *"Much too Much"* ranges?

1. _____

2. _____

3. _____

4. _____

You will use these items in the last chapter, *Designing Your Future,* to begin the creation of a Personal Goal Plan.

Chapter 1 Survey

Avoiding leadership implosion	Much too little		Barely too little		Just right	Barely too much		Much too much	
Please insert an "X" in the appropriate box to indicate your answer	-4	-3	-2	-1	0	+1	+2	+3	+4
How much time do you put into managing your changed relationships with coworkers?									
How many time do you spend working on projects that could be delegated and/or scrapped altogether?									
How much time do you spend thinking about long-term issues affecting the business?									
How much time do you spend involved in running the business?									
How much time do you spend prioritizing the activities in which you are involved?									

Note

1. Smith (2015).

Reference

Smith, J. 2015. "4 Common Reasons Half of All Executives Fail." *Business Insider*. March 2, *www.businessinsider.com/reasons-executives-fail-2015-3.html* (accessed October 26, 2016).

CHAPTER 2

Knowing the Business: Moving from Passenger to Driver

In 2011, CareerBuilder conducted a survey of over 7,500 employees across industries and they found more than two-thirds (68 percent) of employees did not know how much revenue their companies generated each year.[1] According to another study, only 14 percent of employees understand their company's strategy and direction.[2] A Gallup survey found that only 41 percent of employees understand what their company stands for and how their brand is different from their competitors.[3] It is astonishing to learn the extent to which most employees do not understand important aspects of the companies with which they work!

Whether promoted from within or hired from outside the organization, being elevated to a leadership position means treating every aspect of the business *as if it were your own*. This means that you develop such an intimate knowledge of the business that the work you and your team do is clearly tied to those activities involved in making the business more successful. Undoubtedly, it is in the best interest of everyone in the company to make the business more successful, but it is the major part of the leader's job. This paradigm shift in a leader's priorities requires changing from behaving like an employee to *behaving like an owner*, and such a change necessitates developing a greater understanding of the business of your company and ensuring that this knowledge is disseminated clearly throughout your organization.

Contrast this to very successful companies whose leaders regularly communicate to their employees the direction of the company and its values, creating a culture that encourages worker input and innovation. Over the past decade, there have been a handful of companies that have experienced success year-over-year, while their competitors have struggled or failed and gone out of business. Examples include Apple (where are Blackberry and Palm?); Starbucks (in spite of burgeoning mom and pop coffee shops); Amazon (where are Borders and Barnes and Noble?); Netflix (where is Blockbuster?); Nike (still running ahead of Adidas, Puma, and Under Armour); Costco (even with stiff competition from Target, Kroger, and Walmart/Sam's Club). What differentiates these companies from their competitors is a tenacious adherence to their respective strategies and driving these strategies down to all levels in the organization. Not surprisingly, many of these companies are also among the best companies for which to work (Apple, Starbucks, Costco).[4] As a leader, it is important to know your business and how your organization or department measures its success.

In this chapter, we identify the most important business issues that leaders must understand in order to most effectively lead their organizations. These issues are central to the performance of any company, including:

- Understanding a company's business model
- Translating strategy into tactics
- Measuring success

How Does Your Company Make Money?

Leaders need to understand their company's business and *business model*. Every company exists to make money for its owners and stakeholders. A business model must include *how* a company makes money, *who* are its customers and what do the customers *value*. Starbucks sells coffee. Ford sells cars. Microsoft sells software. Apple sells phones and computers. On the surface, this can appear obvious; however, every company has levels of complexity that include things such as advertising, distribution, pricing, inventory, product development and brand recognition.

One business model example is that of Hewlett Packard (HP). HP sells printers at nearly cost, with the expectation that the consumer will buy their very expensive ink cartridges. What good is a printer without the cartridges? HP's profitability is largely in the steep margins of their cartridges. It becomes a recurring revenue model because, like razor blades, each cartridge has a built-in obsolescence depending on the finite amount of ink storage.

Starbucks sells coffee. Its business model is based on *market saturation* with a Starbucks on every corner. The idea is that market saturation and product differentiation *drive* demand instead of creating oversupply. Starbucks has taken having an everyday "cup o' Joe" to a new level. They sell on the basis that their coffee is a *value purchase,* not a commodity. They have created a relaxed environment that is inviting and welcoming. With the added amenities of free Internet and refreshments, millions of people consider their local Starbucks as an attractive place to work, relax, or socialize. This accounts for Starbucks being able to charge high prices for its coffee.

Heinz sells condiments like ketchup, mayonnaise, and pickles. These products are not highly differentiated from the condiments of their competitors. The lower the differentiation between products, the more vulnerable a product is to being commoditized. Commoditized products are sold on the basis of cost, not value. Grocery counters carry several kinds of condiments, including low-cost, privately branded condiments. Shoppers tend to prefer lower price and brand recognition over value in making these purchases.

A company's business model is likely to change over time if market conditions change. IBM began selling tabulating machines. With the onset of computers, it became a seller of hardware, including mainframes and desktop computers. With technology continuing to change, IBM went from punch cards to consulting (its main source of profit today) because it knew it was in the information business, not the punch card business. Western Union began as a telegraph company delivering millions of telegraphs across the world. With the advent of technology, the need for delivering telegraphs became obsolete and Western Union changed its business model, divesting its telegraph business and becoming a worldwide money transfer company.

When we look at a changing business model, Gillette provides a good example. Gillette sells razors, simple enough. Gillette practically gives away its razor handles with the expectation that they will make money on their very expensive fancy blades. After all, what good is a razor handle without blades. Gillette has been one of only two companies (the other being Schick) that has dominated the razor market and, as a result, has been able to charge higher prices. Historically, this model has gone largely unchallenged. However, recently, a new business model has emerged from Dollar Shave Club and Harry's, companies that sell their blades and razor handles online at a steep discount, delivering them directly to your home! Harry's even owns its own manufacturing plant. These companies have essentially changed the paradigm by eliminating the middlemen in the logistics chain (warehousing, delivery, third-party retailers). Table 2.1 provides a comparison of different business models.

As a result of the Dollar Shave Club disruptive model, Gillette's market share and margins have been shrinking. Dollar Shave Club has taken the hassle out of buying razor blades; driving to the store, sorting through a variety of blades, getting the shopkeeper to unlock the display and finally paying a king's ransom for the blades. With its subscription-based online approach, Dollar Shave Club's shave kit, which can include blades, a handle, and shaving cream, arrives in the mailbox of the subscriber on a prearranged just-in-time schedule, with no thought given to all of the hoops through which the buyer previously had to jump. In a defensive maneuver, Gillette has been forced to develop the Gillette Shave Club to try to regain market share.

By knowing a company's business model, a leader can drive the right behaviors in his or her organization for both continuation and sustaining current business success. To understand your company's business model, identify:

- Your produces and services
- Markets in which you sell or compete
- Your customers
- What your customers value
- Activities involved in making products and services (designing, manufacturing, etc.)
- Selling logistics of your products and services (distribution, attracting customers, transacting a sale)
- Your competitors and their market approach

Table 2.1 Business model disruption

Company	Products	End-use customers	Logistics	Distribution	Awareness	Value proposition
Gillette	Razor blades and accessories	Individuals (men and women)	R & D to manufacturer to wholesalers to retailers to customer	Grocery, big box stores, and drug stores	Heavy (and expensive) TV advertising	No-cost handles and high-cost blades, multiple blade options, market domination
Dollar shave company	Razor Blades	Individuals (initially men)	Manufacturer to customer	Internet mail order	Social media (YouTube; Facebook)	Low-cost "system," high volume, few options, subscription based

Running the Organization: Aligning Work to the Business Model

Identifying customers, and what they value, provides companies with an indication of how they need to *operate* to fulfill their business model. The clearer a company is about *how* it is structured to deliver its products and services, the more likely it will be to succeed in its respective markets. Research has determined that companies tend to be focused on one of three areas: operational efficiency, customer intimacy, and product innovation.[5] In order to be successful in an industry, a company must excel in at least one of these areas.

- **Operational efficiency**: In this discipline, a company focuses on tightly managing every aspect of production. This includes cost containment, quality, safety, time to market, inventory control, and operational excellence. In these companies, there is a focus on lean manufacturing to eliminate waste and Six Sigma practices to reduce errors and defects. Companies whose products and services have become commoditized make money on the basis of high-volume/low-cost purchases and must be operationally efficient to be profitable. Their products and services are not significantly differentiated from those of their competitors to warrant a high-value cost. Walk down virtually any supermarket aisle and you will be looking at products from companies that are commoditized. Condiments, sodas, fruits, and vegetables all fall into this category. Manufacturing plants are particularly well suited to adopting an operational efficiency mind-set. An example is the automobile industry where human jobs are being replaced by robots to reduce cost and maximize quality and productivity.

- **Customer intimacy**: Companies with high levels of customer intimacy are characterized by selling on the basis of helping their clients become more successful. This involves a deeper knowledge of customer needs and increasing customer touch points to create customer loyalty. Nordstrom, Zappos, and Amazon are examples of companies that get to know customer's needs and become involved in the delivery to their customers of the specific products and services they desire.

These companies are involved in the total solution of the needs of their customers. Loyalty programs of businesses such as airlines, hotels, and banks are a means of creating such loyalty. Preferences like having soft or firm pillows, a room on a high or low floor, and special concierge services are examples of ways to create customer intimacy.

- **Product leadership**: Companies that are product pace setters in their industries excel in product leadership. Apple is the most obvious company in this category with its regular innovation and search for new ways to attach its customers to its products. BMW is also a company that focuses on product innovation to lure new customers. These companies are characterized by innovation, hiring very good people, giving employees the freedom to create, and being first to market, in spite of the risk of potential product recall or revision.

Once a company understands which of the aforementioned approaches is best suited to their relationships to their customers, they must excel in that approach in order to differentiate from the competition and become, or sustain being, profitable. Each approach requires leaders to provide a different kind of focus for their organizations.

Leadership Implications: From Concept to Practice

In a company that focuses on *operational excellence*, the leader will want to have a leaner organization, a higher focus on creating tightly controlled processes, a limit to independent decisions being made, and the use of practices that control production. This would include practices like lean, Six Sigma, and total quality management (TQM). Important operational practices include having repeatable processes that reduce rework and breakage, keeping inventory to a minimum, maintaining consistent quality, and controlling the on-time distribution to customers. The workforce of an operationally excellent organization will be one that pays attention to detail, tolerates routine, and follows instructions and processes. This requires a mind-set that is highly tactical and able to tolerate routine.

A company focusing on *customer intimacy* will have greater customer contact and understands the customer's needs in more depth than simply selling a product. This requires understanding the customer's specific problems and looking for customized ways to solve them. A leader will want to focus the attention of his/her organization to the needs of the client and create process flexibility to meet changing client needs. Customer intimacy requires a workforce comfortable with client interaction in order to understand customer needs. The mind-set of employees in this organization is flexible, strategic, and relational.

A company focused on *product innovation* will be one that encourages innovation and creativity over processes. These companies are focused on invention, increasing research and development (R&D) cycle times, and comfort using new technologies. They are willing to cannibalize existing products in order to get a jump on the market with the next new product. Workforce in a product innovation company is one that is skilled, highly creative, unbound by either tradition or existing processes, willing to challenge the status quo, and providing room to experiment and fail. Leaders of such organizations are collaborative, more hands-off, and willing to create the kind of culture where innovation is encouraged and failure is not met with punitive consequences, but is seen as a lesson and a step closer to success.

Successful leaders understand the underlying drivers of a company; its markets and customers, products, and services; and how it makes money. However, understanding these things is not enough! A leader must know how to *translate* the drivers of a company into hiring the right kind of people and requiring the kind of behaviors of their employees to support these drivers. Aligning a workforce to the right company drivers requires hiring well, providing well-defined roles and responsibilities, leveraging through delegation, and giving clear direction and accountabilities to drive the right behaviors. Table 2.2 provides such a matrix.

It is important to note that businesses may by competent in more than one of the three disciplines. However, they *must excel* in at least one, in order to be competitive in their space. For example, Starbucks is interested in the customer experience (customer intimacy), it has hundreds of different coffee variations (product innovation), and it is concerned with the costs associated with its logistics (operational excellence). However, the environment it has created for its customers (customer intimacy) is the greatest asset in its business model.

Table 2.2 Leadership implications versus business orientation

Operations	Expectations	Industries	Management practices	Employees
Operational efficiency	Deliver products with consistent quality, low cost, on time, and low complexity	Manufacturing logistics, utilities, transportation, oil and gas, petrochemical	Continuous improvement; focus on quality, productivity, cost, timeliness; compliant	Detail oriented, tolerate routine, highly tactical, process rule-adherent, diligent, dutiful
Customer intimacy	Tailored and customized solutions for customers	Airlines, hotels, lifestyle products, retail, banking	Customer knowledge and understanding for broad solutions; long-term relationships,	Relational, analytic, diligent, flexible, curious
Product leadership	Creative and unique products and services	High tech, automotive, investments, pharmaceuticals.	Innovative and inventive, strategic, teamwork, comfortable with failure	Creative, collaborative, flexible and willing to experiment

Case Study

Growing the Business by Engaging the Workforce

One of our clients was a 40-year-old manufacturing firm that was clear about the products it sold, the markets into which they were sold, and their end-use customers. Over a two-year period, it saw its profits declining and it had gone from being an industry leader to being "in the middle of the pack." Its margins were shrinking and its cash flow was being squeezed. More troubling was that its sales were continuing at a decent pace. As the company leaders further analyzed their financials, they noticed that their manufacturing costs had begun to soar. They realized that they had not educated their workforce about the metrics of the business, including how the company made money and how it managed costs. At an all-company meeting, they enlisted the help of the workforce to better manage costs of manufacturing.

(Continued)

Immediately after the meeting, the operations manager posted a series of graphs related to manufacturing. The graphs were posted in the lunch room, in hallways, and on the manufacturing floor. These graphs displayed the various aspects of the manufacturing process, including waste, quality, breakage, time to market, inventory control, and materials management. Every week the graphs were updated and the entire manufacturing organization reviewed progress on every item. This created a bit of healthy competition between departments to lower cost. Within a relatively short period, the organization's productivity improved dramatically. Manufacturing costs came increasingly under control and the company's profitability began to rise again. An unexpected benefit was that the morale on the manufacturing floor improved dramatically, as did retention. When questioned about this difference, employees said that they had begun to feel a pride that they made a difference in the success of the company. Management took note and identified additional ways to involve employees in the life of the business.

Leadership by the Numbers: Knowing When You are Winning

The value of an effective business model and tactics to implement it are usually found in the company's scorecard: profitability. We say *usually* because, in this dot-com era, companies that are not profitable are occasionally bought and sold at premiums that defy logic. However, for most companies, the bottom line is a good indicator of the effectiveness of their strategy and the execution of their tactics. There are several metrics about which every leader needs to become knowledgeable. In sports, you do not know if you are winning if you do not keep score. In business, you will not know if the business is successful if you are not familiar with the metrics that define success or failure. Furthermore, the more transparent these metrics are to the workforce, and the more educated employees are about them, the greater the likelihood that the metrics will help drive their behaviors. While there is an almost infinite number of metrics, a few metrics best indicate the overall health of the business.

Revenue

The total gross amount of income a company makes from sales of goods and services is the revenue number. It can also include interest income from investments. Revenue is a broad indicator of the growth of a business. However, it is not the best indicator of the *health* of the business. Revenue can increase because of rising prices of products, acquisitions, new market entry, and other unusual streams. However, it is the income from goods and services that is the most important indicator of growth. Looking at long-term trends provides a better understanding of sustained growth.

Profit

The amount of money left over after a company's costs are taken from the gross revenue constitutes its profits. Costs include overhead like personnel, office space, payments on assets, one-time costs associated with acquisitions, R&D or new market entry, and the like. Profit is often referred to as earnings before interest and taxes (EBIT) or earnings before interest, taxes, depreciation, and amortization (EBITDA). Occasionally, a company has a high profit that is an aberration through the sale of a business or the unexpected customer adoption of a new product. Viewing profitability over time is a better way to determine the strength of a company.

Cash Flow

The inflow and outflow of money from a business are its operating cash flow. Cash flow is necessary for the daily operations of a business, including taxes, purchasing inventory, and operating costs. Having healthy cash flow is critical to keeping a company in business. It helps pay debts and salaries for employees. Companies with strong sales but delinquent accounts receivable can get into cash-flow problems, in spite of their growth. This often happens with businesses that grow too fast and let their cost commitments exceed their ability to collect revenue. Free cash flow (FCF) is the cash a company is able to generate after covering its costs. FCF is essential in helping a business increase its offerings of goods and services, increase R&D costs, and continuously improve its operating systems. FCF represents the true profitability of a business.

Operating Margins

When selling goods and services, the operating margin is the *percentage of gain* after accounting for the costs of the goods and services. A company's operating margins are the best indicator of the health of a business. Operating margins are only meaningful in the context of the industry in which the company competes. It is not unusual for grocery stores to have an operating margin of only 1 percent. Industries that specialize in human capital like accounting firms and legal services can have operating margins of over 15 percent. A company can look at its operating margins in two ways. First, are the company's operating margins compared to the industry average? Second, are the company's operating margins increasing or decreasing?

Market Share

Market share is the degree to which a company's goods and services have penetrated the markets in which they compete. Considering that every market has a 100 percent amount of goods and services to be sold in a market, what percentage of that 100 percent does a company have. The higher the percentage, the more market share a company has. However, this can be a tricky number because it is not always related to profitability. HEB grocers in Texas had a market strategy of going into new markets and, for a period of time, underselling competitors with the hope that they would develop a customer base and hurt, or drive out, the competition. They were willing to initially "buy" a market at a loss with the goal of having a strong profitable long-term presence.

There are any number of other metrics that can be followed and are useful. Stock price and price fluctuation, return on assets, and return on equity are such metrics. These can all help leaders make business decisions. Understanding the key metrics that we have outlined will give every leader sufficient information to make business decisions by studying the numbers to better understand what they mean and make changes accordingly. Understanding, and communicating, these metrics is not simply an academic exercise, but is essential in creating a culture in which leaders develop a sense of urgency and engagement among their employees that contributes to the success of the business.

Coach's Corner

In this chapter, we have emphasized the importance of leaders acting like owners and having a very well-developed understanding of how their companies make money. For leaders to be most effective, they need to be able to connect the work of the people in their organizations to the overall objectives and direction of the company.

Essentials for Understanding Your Business

1. **Business model**: Leaders need to understand how their businesses make money. This understanding includes understanding a business's goods and services, end-use customers, logistics of product or service delivery, and its value proposition. In addition, leaders need to communicate this business model throughout their organizations to create a sense of connection and urgency in the workforce.

2. **Company discipline**: Once the business model is well understood, leaders need to focus on aligning how the business makes money to its internal operating processes. This alignment will help sustain the company's business model in the markets in which it competes.

3. **Understanding the numbers**: The success of any business is measured primarily by a few key metrics. These metrics inform leaders about the overall health of the company and where additional attention is required. Understanding, and sharing, these metrics helps everyone in the company feel a part of the success of the business.

Chapter 2 Survey

Business acumen	Much too little		Barely too little		Just right	Barely too much		Much too much	
	−4	−3	−2	−1	0	+1	+2	+3	+4
Please insert an "X" in the appropriate box to indicate your answer									
To what extent do you understand your company's business model?									
To what extent have you used this understanding in creating an effective organization?									
How well are people in your organization able to connect their work to the business model?									

Areas for Development

What are the top three ways you can become a more effective leader by better understanding your company?

1. _____

2. _____

3. _____

Notes

1. Careerbuilder (2012).
2. Schiemann (2009).
3. Fleming and Witters (2012).
4. Bort (2015).
5. Treacy and Wiersema (1995).

References

Bort, J. 2015. "The 50 Best Places To Work In 2016 According To Employees." *Business Insider,* December 9. *www.businessinsider.com/50-best-places-to-work-in-2016-2015-12* (accessed March 21, 2017).

Careerbuilder. 2012. *http://careerbuilder.com/Share/AboutUs/IndustryTrends.aspx?archiveyear=2012* (accessed March 24, 2017).

Fleming, J.H., and D. Witters. 2012. "Your Employees Don't 'Get' Your Brand." *Gallup Business Journal,* July 26. *http://gallup.com/businessjournal/156197/Employees-Don-Brand.aspx* (accessed on March 26, 2017).

Schiemann, W. 2009. "Aligning Performance Management with Organizational Strategy, Values, and Goals." In *Performance Management: Putting Research into action,* eds. J.W. Smither and M. London. San Francisco: Josey-Bass.

Treacy, M., and Wiersema, F. 1995. *Discipline of Market Leaders.* Addison-Wesley.

CHAPTER 3

Setting a Vision: Avoiding the Fog of Tomorrow

In September 2012, Best Buy brought in Hubert Joly as its new chief executive officer (CEO). He had been the CEO of Carlson, a global hospitality and travel company. At the time, it seemed as though Best Buy had lost its way. Best Buy had experienced a steady decline in sales with competition from Amazon and others. Shortly after Joly was brought into Best Buy their stock hit an all-time low of $10.91. Staff morale was low and many anticipated the worst. There was speculation that hiring Joly was a mistake.

Joly spent three months in the depths of the organization, working in stores, meeting customers, and understanding their needs. As a result, he reset Best Buy's vision known as "Renew Blue." He refocused the company on technical service and solutions, and creating new stores with a friendlier shopping environment. He also vowed to match Amazon's low pricing while providing superior customer service and product selection. As a result of his *Renew Blue* strategy, staff morale improved, productivity increased, and earnings improved. At a time when many competitors like Circuit City or Radio Shack were going out of business or scaling down, Best Buy has flourished. Since then, under Joly's leadership, Best Buy's stock has risen to over $49 per share in December 2016, a truly amazing turnaround.[1]

What Joly accomplished in a 4-year period was a result of his clear and unrelenting focus, one that led to a well-defined Best Buy strategy that all employees could rally around. His ability to understand what customers wanted and anticipate where the market was headed resulted in a new, improved company.

Leadership and Vision Setting: Guiding the Ship

It is common for employees in organizations to be either unfamiliar with, or unaware of, their company's business strategy. This is often true even at the top levels of organizations! It is estimated that only 14 percent of employees understand their company's strategy and direction.[2] It is no wonder that once a company reaches a certain level of growth, it is difficult to grow beyond that stage. The direction the leaders have set is either undeveloped or too vague.

Company leaders are notorious for either *continuing* to do what they were doing in previous jobs, *repeating* what the previous person in that position had done, or going in a completely new and unfamiliar direction that is out of sync with the organization. In addition, new leaders often lack the courage or security in their positions to clarify what they do not understand or to challenge norms when they believe a company's direction is poorly thought out. A leader cannot communicate a vision in the midst of this fog of misunderstanding, vagueness, and lack of clarity. Through our evaluations, we have found that there are three typical approaches new leaders follow to creating a vision. Before a leader can set an effective vision, he or she must know where the ship is headed.

The Timid Leader

An exploratory vessel on its way to the Arctic circle jerks to a stop. The ship has become frozen in a thick layer of ice. If the vessel turns back it abandons its scientific mission and calls into question the viability of future missions. Failure is to be avoided at all costs. The ship's captain decides to wait out the storm and consider all options. Meanwhile the ice is mounting, freezing the ship in place. As the hours tick by, the captain slowly mulls over possible solutions to the ship's fate. Ice clings to the rigging, the mast, and the crow's nest, yet the captain still hesitates to act. Worse yet, the captain orders the crew to continue their duties as usual, stoking coal and washing the deck as if the ship is not freezing in narrow straits. The ship is too burdened to continue. The mission is lost.

In the aforementioned scenario, the captain does little or nothing in the way of providing a vision to the ship's crew. In business, whether looking one year ahead or five years ahead, ice is always encroaching in the form of changing markets and competition. The *timid leader* is one who simply falls in step and has all employees in their charge continue to do what they have been doing. These leaders are characterized by reinforcing the practices, processes, and procedures that are in place, no matter how antiquated or misaligned they may be. Such leaders tend to be wedded to the past and what they already know, in large measure because of their fear of making a mistake. Their leadership is characterized by looking in the rearview mirror, while believing that they are looking into the future. They are fearful of looking forward because the future is unfamiliar and potentially frightening. Ultimately, they operate at a tactical level well below their leadership pay grade. They expect obedience to the way things have been done and provide little direction for the reality of the situation.

These timid leaders often work diligently and dutifully to complete tasks and they are very tactical in nature. They just do things on their own, not trusting easily, and often work in isolation from their own direct reports, providing very little direction or counsel. Their primary concern is to not make mistakes. Their tendency to become isolated and uncommunicative leaves their direct reports operating in a vacuum. The backroom description of these leaders is that they are weak-willed and lack backbone. Any vision they attempt to provide is simply a tactical picture of the past, lacking creativity or inspiration. In fact, it is no vision at all.

As Chinese strategist and philosopher Sun Tzu observed, "tactics without strategy is the noise before defeat."[3] By being wedded to the past, we co-opt the future. While it is tactics that keep an organization functioning in the present, leaders must develop a telescopic view of the landscape to secure the future. The longer-term vision provides a plan for the future for the organization. The more a leader is involved in tactics, the more risk an organization has of losing its way. Danger ahead!!!

The Overbearing Leader

On another expedition, our Arctic explorers stagger to a halt in the ice once again. A new captain is at the helm of the ship. Without a second thought this captain orders the crew into action. A quarter of the crew is sent directly onto the ice floes to hack away at the ice by hand. Another quarter is sent off over the ice to search for alternate routes north. Yet another quarter of the crew is tasked with spreading lit kindling out over the frozen ocean. The rest of the crew remains on deck and bellows obscenities into the wind, just because. The snow continues to fall, separating the crew and putting out their fires. The ice continues to mount in spite of the flurry of action. Separated, they have become ineffectual. With crew members scattered to the four winds the mission is lost.

This second captain runs into the equally detrimental pitfall of becoming overconfident, riding the wave of the momentum created by his or her ascendency. This type of *overbearing leader* provides a daring, but completely ineffective, vision to his or her organization. This brashness is an outcome of them trying to prove the wisdom of their having been put into a position of leadership. Such an overly bold vision can be as harmful as the one of the timid leader who presents no vision at all. These audacious leaders believe they are looking through a window to the future, with little regard for the past. Unlike the *timid leader* who can be stuck in the past, these overbearing leaders are intent on *running from the past* to the future without regard to previous lessons learned.

Overbearing leaders typically dominate their organizations and require their employees to follow them blindly, even when they are on a path to ruin. The overbearing leader's behavior is often very directive, sometimes charismatic, but not encouraging of either collaboration or counsel. They tend to act with a sense of urgency, listen too little, and provide scant detail with their mandates. They have no problems working around company rules or policies in order to accomplish their goals. The vision they present is often conceptual and lacking in clarity with little, if any, apparent alignment to the overall strategy of the company. The backbiting comments about such leaders are that they unwisely press onward through the fog. At a time when the leader should "not just do something, but stand there," they do something impulsive that is the wrong something to do. Such a vision is really an untethered fantasy, neither undergirded with the learnings of the past nor guided by the reality of the future. Again, to quote philosopher Sun Tzu, "strategy without tactics is the slowest road to victory." Mistaking grandiosity for productivity is a sure path to irrelevance.

The behaviors of the *timid leader* and the *overbearing leader* have a similar root cause—personal insecurity and lack of maturity. The two types exhibit opposite ways of compensating for those feelings. At both extremes, the impact on the organization is negative. Feelings of insecurity are not just the domain of ineffective leaders. There are times and situations when even the most genuinely secure person will feel apprehensive and anxious.

"My last comment 'appeared' to be inviting feedback. Do not be fooled."

Figure 3.1 Feedback?

Source: andrewgenn/Depositphotos.com. http://depositphotos.com/19051135/stock-photo-boss-makes-it-clear-he.html (accessed November 20, 2016).

It is part of being human to experience moments of personal discomfort, especially when confronted with new and unfamiliar challenges. The question is not whether leaders will feel bouts of insecurity, but how they will react *when* they have them. What distinguishes leaders who are effective in setting a vision from those who are not is *how* they deal with these bouts of uncertainty and self-doubt.

The Goldilocks Leader

Our ship comes to halt once again. This time, a completely different captain is in command. The captain calmly consults the ship's officers, their sextant, and a weather forecast. With this information, the captain orders half the crew to chip away at the ice floes that have trapped the vessel. The other half of the crew navigates the vessel and assists from onboard. It is not easy going, but little by little the ice is chipped away from the sides of the ship. The crew shimmies back onboard and, with a loud squelch, the ship comes free from the ice altogether. Slowly, our Arctic explorers press on into the distance. Mission accomplished!

The approach of this third captain, and the one that is used by the most effective leaders in setting a vision, is characterized by far different behaviors from the previous captains. In this approach, you find a calm, mature leader who knows that emotional ups and downs are a part of life. This leader is neither timid nor brash as he or she directs, inspires, and motivates his or her team. Such leaders maintain composure while setting a clear direction for their mission.

Effective leaders neither shirk from their leadership responsibilities nor do they become overpowering. They balance listening with talking, reflecting with taking action, and acknowledging the past with embracing the future. These mature leaders have learned that their primary responsibility is to provide direction for their organizations that balances the strategy of the future with the tactics of the present. They focus on creating a picture of the future of their organizations in which each person understands how his or her job is linked to the ultimate success of the business.

There are several keys to *beginning* the process of mature and effective vision development:

- **Managing feelings**: Leaders must become aware of, and manage, the periodic emotional spikes they experience when they feel overwhelmed.
- **Collaborating**: Leaders must engage with influential and informed colleagues to identify a future path that is best for continued business success.
- **Setting agendas**: Leaders must become dedicated to setting agendas that are focused and disciplined.
- **Working on the strategy**: Leaders must insist that the management team spend a substantial amount of time developing a vision for their company, rather than only reacting to the crisis of the day.
- **Managing outcomes**: Detailing metrics about how to measure the success or failure of outcomes is both necessary and critical. How will you be able to claim either to have succeeded or failed?

By adhering closely to these keys, leaders can set a framework for developing a transparent vision that becomes the foundation on which a business thrives.

Becoming a Periscopic Leader

Now that we have a framework for creating a vision, how do we begin to think about establishing a vision? Consider the submarine. One of the key strategic advantages of submarines is their periscope. Periscopes have long been used in order to see the objects that are not in direct line of sight. From inside the submarine, deep under the water's surface, objects above water cannot be viewed without the help of periscopes. A periscope has no utility for seeing inside a submarine, only outside. This serves as a metaphor for the developing leader. It is not enough to see inside the company to identify areas for greater effectiveness, cost control, and operational efficiencies. A company can quickly reach the point of diminishing returns even when processes are well honed and manufacturing is operating at an extraordinarily high level of efficiency.

The leader must look *outside* the company to find other competitive advantages. Opportunities can include:

- Innovation
- Technological changes
- Changes in the makeup of customer demography
- Regulatory and legal compliance changes
- Economic aberrations

To continue to look inside the company for constant improvement, without looking outside into the marketplace, is like having a submarine with no periscope—a futile and potentially deadly situation! *The leader must become the periscope*! Becoming a periscope provides three potential benefits that are essential to crafting an organization's vision.

You Cannot Address What You Cannot (or Will Not) See

The first benefit of looking outside your company is seeing the obvious. It does no good to scan the external environment, market, or trends when you have no intention of considering alternative ways of conducting your business. When companies either fail or refuse to look at the environment outside of their companies, they run the risk of creating the conditions for their own demise. While companies can be content to be fast-followers as opposed to first-to-market, they must be willing to make necessary changes to continue to compete. Identifying opportunities and making changes become the responsibility of the leader. Consider the case of Kodak.

In 1975, when Kodak engineer Steve Sasson invented the first digital camera, Kodak commanded an overwhelming majority of the camera and film sales markets in the United States. Not wanting to jeopardize their market share, Kodak shelved the technology. As Sasson later recalled, "It was filmless photography, so management's reaction was, 'that's cute—but don't tell anyone about it.'"[4] Kodak missed an obvious opportunity to be an early adopter of what would unequivocally become the future of photography. Today the company's market share is dismal. Either no one was willing to be Kodak's "periscope" or a lens cap was covering their periscope, hiding its ability to view the landscape.

The rate of change in technology is causing disruption in industry after industry. Where is Blockbuster? The Encyclopedia Britannica? What is happening to Circuit City? Ultimately, these failures are not about technological changes, but they are about the inability of leaders to identify the challenges ahead and adapt accordingly. Obviously, the larger the company the slower and less able it will be to change course. However, the submarine is put in a perilous position when no one is looking through the periscope.

Some would argue that identifying opportunities is nothing more than seeing the obvious from the eyes of the customer! The seeds of a company's destruction are sown when it becomes rigorously and stubbornly wedded to how it has been successful in the past. Once you hear that a company is "refocusing on its core" you begin to suspect the company is, or is about to be, in trouble. When creating a vision, the savvy leader would be wise to look beyond what has made his or her company successful in the past to what the customers and market are wanting in the future.

Spotting Mines in the Ocean: Anticipating Challenges and Opportunities

The second benefit of the leader as periscope is early identification of challenges and opportunities. The visionary leader will use his or her vantage point to *anticipate changes* rather than to react to them. Much like spotting dangers through a periscope, the leader needs to proactively identify opportunities and challenges ahead. The leader needs to detect what the company will be *facing in the future*. Examples of such future trends include:

Cybersecurity: According to the Verizon Data Breach Investigations Reports, over 700 million records were exposed due to data breaches in 2014 alone. How will your business be forced to change in an ever more networked and by extension hackable world?

Industry-specific roadblocks: Because of reduced power plant emission requirements as a result of climate change regulation, the 2015 coal production was at its lowest level since 1986.[5] This has resulted in the loss of over 400,000 jobs. How will your industry be impacted by a changing climate and political landscape?

Institutional memory: The Georgetown University's Center for Education and Workforce determined that two-thirds of jobs that open up to college graduates are a result of retirement.[6] This results in a loss of institutional information. What is your company doing to retain the information in the face of these retiring employees?

All future trends are available to every company; *they are not a secret*. Internet searches can identify them readily and quickly. It is not that a leader will have information not available to the competition, but it is how imaginatively and proactively the leader creates strategies to deal with these changes that sets the front runners from the laggards. It is common for companies to have "skunkworks" teams, whose entire responsibility is to look at trends and the white space we discussed earlier. This trend-spotting strategy should be a part of any business that hopes to expand and sustain its success, and it should be factored into any strategic vision.

Eyes on the Competition: When Second Place Is Really Best

The third benefit of taking a look at the broader business environment is being able to identify ways to hasten the distribution and adoption of new products. One short-cut strategy is to focus relentlessly on the competition and identify their early marketplace successes and failures. There are times when being a fast-follower is a more successful strategy than being a first-mover. First-movers are characterized by being first to market with new products and services, with the hope of preempting the competition. The motivation behind first-movers is that by getting a jump on the competition, their products and services can become more quickly adopted by customers and thus dominate a market. There are times when this is true, such as when Amazon started by aggressively building the "World's Largest Bookstore," and then extending its brand to other verticals.

However, it can be an even bigger advantage to *observe* the reaction of customers to these first-movers as well as to identify early problems or issues with both products and early adoption of customers. Fast-followers are ready to follow the lead of successful products and services without having either the research and development (R&D) costs or the risk to profitability. But their reaction must be quick to prevent the first-mover from turning an early success into market domination. Successful fast-follower companies include Zantac and Google. Zantac, a later entry into the ulcer drug market, but with fewer side effects than competing drugs, became the largest selling prescription drug in the world. Google was not the first search engine but had time to work out kinks identified in earlier search engines to master that space.

Research has suggested that first-movers have a 47 percent failure rate while fast-followers have only an 8 percent failure rate.[7] Fast-followers pay intense and ongoing attention to competitors and the products and services they bring to the market. They watch things like customer adoption, feature problems, and potential adjacent markets—all without having to burn through cash on R&D. Much can be learned by carefully observing the response to a new and potentially disruptive product.

Magnifying Glass or Binoculars: Creating a Vision

The central purpose of creating a vision is to make it possible for all employees under a leader's charge clearly understand where the company is headed and their role in helping the company get there. Any other information is superfluous to this end. Maximizing the talent in the organization to perform at the highest level of productivity is the ultimate objective. It is the leader's primary role to provide employees this clarity of direction, communicate it throughout his or her organization, create metrics for identifying progress toward the end goal, and align people's roles and responsibilities toward succeeding in this environment.

When setting a vision, it is a common mistake to confuse tactics for strategy. This is particularly true for leaders who have emerged from the operations side of a business. Their ascent into leadership roles has often been characterized by being exceptional project managers, supervisors, or product engineers. Creating Gantt charts, spreadsheets, and schedules has been their bread and butter. They have been rewarded by their team's success in accomplishing a series of tasks for quarterly or annual success. Naturally, for these folks, setting a vision is about next quarter, not next year or five years out. Strategy for them becomes a series of tactics that go out into the future, without considering external circumstances that may require them to think, and behave, fundamentally differently. Leaders need to guard against falling prey to setting strategy based on what happened in the past (rearview mirror strategy); or focusing on continuous improvement of what exists currently as a strategic foundation. (The light bulb was not invented by continuously improving the candle.) In our work with successful executives, we have found some unique ways they follow for strategy creation.

Give Your Organization HUGS Goals

Identifying what will really move their organization into the future is the most important focal point for a new leader. Whether running a function or becoming a new CEO, the leader's job is to recognize opportunities for, and manage, change. In today's world, according to Industry Tap, the rate of knowledge doubles every 13 months. Leaders must become *proactive* learners, discontent with yesterday's successes. In crafting a compelling vision, the most successful leaders adhere to the HUGS principle. HUGS is an acronym for: huge, ubiquitous, groundbreaking, and strategic.

- **Huge**: By definition, a vision is not much of a vision if it does not require those in the organization to squint or figuratively use binoculars to see where you are wanting to lead them. This is not simply another annual plan that represents year-over-year incremental growth. These leaders create ambitious goals and/or very compressed timelines that serve as a call to action! These huge goals carry a higher risk–reward ratio and are not for everyone. These goals are exhilarating, inspiring and, at times, a little daunting. These courageous leaders know that mobilizing an organization can best be accomplished when everyone is required to perform his or her very best, on an ongoing basis, on a large important initiative that benefits everyone.

- **Ubiquitous**: Periscope leaders know that their ambitious goals must have a broad impact in the organization. They are not simply trying to elevate their function or business unit. Their goals have the potential of lifting the entire organization to a new and higher level. When these goals are set, others in the organization see them as potentially synergistic and recognize the potential value to all. They are truly win–win targets.

- **Groundbreaking**: The more disruptive the huge goal, the greater the potential it has to impact the marketplace. The best way to upend a competitor is to do the unexpected. As we discussed earlier, this does not require the company to be the first to market. It does require the product, service, or process to solve a customer problem in a manner that represents a marked improvement over that to which they are accustomed. Be prepared that this can be disruptive both internally and externally.

- **Strategic**: Perhaps most importantly, the huge goal must be in the *best future interest* of the company. A goal that is large, widespread, and disruptive, but does not benefit the company, can tilt the risk–reward ratio to a risky failure. This strategic planning requires the collaboration of internal critical thinkers, a study of the potential in the marketplace, and, possibly, the counsel of external sources. Because the goal is huge, ubiquitous, and groundbreaking means it should not be created in haste or in the absence of reasonable study. This is not "the flavor of the day!"

The successful leader will understand that at the top of his or her agenda is the creation of a vision that will look forward and involve key individuals inside and outside the organization. The successful leader must have the courage to change the course, if not the history, of the business!

Case Study

Broom Closet to Penthouse

A privately held, family-owned, manufacturing firm in the automobile and computer parts business had a long history of making decent revenue, but only margins of about 2 percent in a growing market. They took a risk and appointed the first nonfamily member as president. The new president had been a long-time employee of the organization, having begun as a janitor. He had only a high school education but had moved up through the sales organization becoming the top salesman year-over-year. Once he became president, we helped him set a HUGS goal for the company: 20 percent earnings before interest and taxes (EBIT). This goal was adopted and incentivized by all parts of the company from the floor laborers to the supervisors, and quality, sales, and distribution staff. This strategy was communicated and translated throughout the organization. Employees quickly identified how, in their jobs, they could make a difference to contribute to this goal. They looked at processes from reducing breakage, increasing timely delivery, maximizing quality, and developing a "just in time" approach reducing inventory. He maintained this simple strategy without any major changes. In the space of three years, the company doubled revenue and increased EBIT to the 20 percent goal set forth by the president. By keeping the goal a simple, but critical one, every employee began to align his or her roles and behaviors to the company's goal, making needed changes and becoming determined to accomplish it. This is a real testament to the HUGS principle!

Occam Was Right: Simpler Is Better

In their quest to be noticed and make a difference, new leaders often make things more complex than is necessary. They try to apply the skills that previously made them successful in solving short-term, tactical problems, to creating longer-term plans. This is another case in which what works at a tactical, operational level, does not work at a more strategic level.

In 1347, William of Ockham developed what has been referred to as the law of parsimony. The most current translation of this is that *the simplest explanation is usually the best one*. The more complex or numerous the explanations or goals, the less likely they are to be testable and achievable. In fact, we can focus on only a few major things at a time. When presented with too many major things simultaneously, we tend not to accomplish any of them. In fact, the Covey organization has determined that the more goals an organization has, the less likely it is to accomplish them, as illustrated in Figure 3.2.[8]

# of Goals	1–3	4–10	11–20
Goals successfully completed	1–3	1–2	0

Figure 3.2 Goals vs. achievement

The most effective leaders are able to identify the very few objectives that will make the greatest difference in their organization and have their team focus on those. When leaders identify those few, high-impact goals, they are more likely to be accomplished and have the greatest impact on the success of the function or business. Along with the identification of three or less HUGS, the leader needs to put into place a process of measuring the success of the huge goal. This begins with the assignment of an owner of the goal who is expected to put a team in place to accomplish the goal. The leader will want to create a dashboard for the goal that includes timelines for phases of completion; metrics to review the quality and quantities the goal is expected to achieve; a process to escalate and resolve issues that surface; and rewards or consequences when specific milestones or targets are or are not met. The leader will also want to put into place a regular review process for his or her team to discuss the dashboard.

Sound the Foghorn: Communicate, Communicate, Communicate

Accomplishing an objective the size of a HUGS initiative requires the entire organization to get behind it. The absolute best outcome, like the one in our case study, is when all employees, at the every level, can see as direct a line between their daily work and the contribution they make to the overall accomplishment of the goal. Imagine employees coming to work every day with the belief

Figure 3.3 Communication

Source: andrewgenn/Depositphotos.com. http://depositphotos.com/60466587/stock-illustration-sounds-kooky.html (accessed November 28, 2016).

that they are making a meaningful contribution to the future success of the company. This requires creating comprehensive communication vehicles for leaders and managers to engage employees in the accomplishment of the goal. This is not a time to be overly subtle or cautious. Inform all involved about the criticalness of achieving the goal and the potential consequences of not achieving it.

Managers at every level carry the burden of *translating* a vision into tactics and making roles and responsibilities clear to their subordinates. This means that leaders have the responsibility for systematically breaking down HUGS initiatives into increasingly tactical objectives and actions. This process requires attention to detail, persistence, and courage to overcome internal obstacles. The most senior leaders have the responsibility of driving the HUGS through the organization, communicating regularly, making revisions as necessary, and keeping momentum alive. Most companies have "graveyards of initiatives" that were a twinkle in someone's eye but did not have the full support of management throughout the organization to get them completed. Nothing is more detrimental to company morale than to have an announcement of yet another new "flavor-of-the-day" initiative, only to have it die after great expense and manpower have gone into it.

Creating a comprehensive communication plan for the duration of the project is essential to ensure that work on the initiative is kept alive and that employees at every level continue to have an understanding of the focus of their work. A communication plan will have the following elements:

- Identifying the goal of each communication
- Identifying the audience (different for each level)
- Developing the messages
- Selecting communication channels
- Identifying spokesperson(s)
- Establishing a timeline
- Executing on the plan

Not only must leaders polish off their foghorns, they must also use them regularly and in a sustained manner until the completion of the initiative.

The Compass and the Map: Vision-Setting Process

A compass provides the general direction for a person, team, or organization to head. A map fills in the blanks providing longitude, latitude, and greater specificity. Often an organization's vision stops at the compass stage, leaving too much variation for interpretation—are we going due north, northwest, or northeast? In order for an organization to fulfill its vision, there needs to be a greater level of detail that points everyone not only in the right direction, but to the exact location. Leaders must provide a clear vision that everyone in their organization understands and can articulate. It is this vision that directs the daily work of all individuals. The most effective leaders do this through:

1. Understanding context: Spending adequate time developing an understanding of the opportunities and challenges that an organization currently faces is prerequisite to taking action.
2. Collaborating: Identify those in the organization or business who have unique and intelligent perspectives and work with them to begin creating a plan.

3. Surveying the landscape: As a major part of the data collection process, the leader needs to look within and outside of his or her organization to see where the organization can go and where it should go.

4. Creating a vision: With the information at hand, the leader and his or her lieutenants can begin using HUGS to create a plan for the future. Keep the plan simple, only three or less very important goals and objectives, consistently focused on what will make the greatest difference.

5. Communicating: Once the leader and the senior team have created a vision, pain needs to be taken to ensure that the plan is communicated throughout all levels of the organization. A vision will only be achieved if everyone is able to see and embrace it.

By following this process, leaders and their organizations can be assured of pulling in the same direction and dramatically increasing the likelihood of company success.

Coach's Corner

A unified vision is critical to the success of any organization. This vision must be actionable and garner the support of individuals at every level of the organization. It is apparent that the more clarity leaders can provide their organizations, the better the organizations will perform.

Three Tips for Creating a Vision

1. **Be a Goldilocks Leader**
   • Resist the temptation to either ride the inertia of the organization you lead or prove yourself by forcing through too many new and erratic initiatives. Find the middle path and set a confident vision through consultation and collaboration.

2. **Become a Periscope**
   • Look outside your organization to identify major trends in the market and among competitors. Without this vital information, it is impossible to set a successful vision.

Chapter 3 Survey

Avoiding the fog of tomorrow	Much too little	Barely too little	Just right	Barely too much	Much too much	
Please insert an "X" in the appropriate box to indicate your answer	−4	−3	−2	−1	0	+1	+2	+3	+4
How often do you initiate actions outside of your organization's previous scope?									
How many goals do you set for your organization?									
How often do you monitor market trends?									
How often do you monitor your competition?									

3. Limit Your Goals

- The best and most successfully executed visions are the simplest. Keep your goals narrowly focused and achievable to ensure that your organization does not flounder in uncertainty. Choose one to three that are central to your vision.

Areas for Development

As you think about your company, what are the top three goals or objectives that are critical to the current and long-term success to the organization?

1. _____

2. _____

3. _____

Notes

1. Loeb (2016).
2. Schiemann (2009).
3. Art of War Quotes (2016).
4. Mui (2012).
5. Annual Coal Report (2016).
6. Carnevale, Smith, and Strohl (2013).
7. Golder and Tellis (1993).
8. McChesney, Covey, and Huling (2012).

References

Annual Coal Report 2016. U.S. Energy information Administration. Release Date: November 3, *www.eia.gov/coal/annual/* (accessed November 20, 2016).

Art of War Quotes. 2016. *www.artofwarquotes.com* (accessed November 2016).

Carnevale, A.P., N. Smith, and J. Strohl. 2013. "Recovery: Job Growth and Education Requirements Through 2020." Georgetown University's Center for Education and Workforce, June 2013 at *https://cew.georgetown.edu/wcontent/uploads/2014/Recovery2020* (accessed November 28, 2016).

Golder, P.N., and G.J. Tellis. 1993. "Pioneer Advantage: Marketing Logic or Marketing Legend?." *Journal of Marketing Research* 30, no. 2, pp. 158–170.

Loeb, W. 2016. "My Retailer of The Year: CEO Hubert Joly Puts The Best In Best Buy." *Forbes*, December 26. *http://forbes.com/sites/walterloeb/2016/12/26/2017-retailer-of-the-year-ceo-hubert-joly-puts-the-best-in-best-buy/.html* (accessed January 5, 2017).

McChesney, C., S. Covey, and J. Huling. 2012. *The 4 Disciplines of Execution.* New York: Simon & Schuster.

Mui, C. 2012. "How Kodak Failed." *Forbes Leadership*, Jan 18. *www.forbes.com/sites/chunkamui/2012/01/18/how-kodak-failed* (accessed November 2016).

Schiemann, W. 2009. "Aligning Performance Management with Organizational Strategy, Values, and Goals." In *Performance Management: Putting Research into Action,* ed. J.W. Smither, et. al., 45–88. San Francisco: Josey-Bass.

CHAPTER 4

Effective Delegation: Trusting Others Not to Steal Your Wallet

Executives moving into leadership positions are initially likely to have the "drinking from a firehose" experience. New leaders can be so overwhelmed with the demands of their position, learning the business, and meeting the people for whom they are responsible, that just sorting through tasks and initiatives is daunting. These issues are compounded dramatically when the leader has come from outside the organization. While new leaders *always* need help in the management of duties, it is not always clear who and what they should include in this process.

This is not an issue that is isolated to new leaders. In fact, the Change Management Consulting organization has estimated that only 40 percent of all managers know how to delegate effectively.[1] These figures mirror our work with leaders, who often struggle with successfully delegating work. Because leaders are often promoted on the basis of their past successes and individual efforts, they may feel the need to continue doing it all themselves. This is especially true of first-time managers, but can also be the case with more senior executives who have high

Figure 4.1 Leadership Leverage[2]

Source: michaeldb/Depositphotos.com.http://deposit-photos.com/7832196/tock-illustration-one-business-man-worth-his.html (accessed December 10, 2016).

control needs. In any case, one of the biggest challenges for leaders is to leverage themselves through the work and capabilities of those who work for them.

Delegation for Productivity: Magnifying Results by Leveraging Leadership

Leaders are promoted into management positions because their organization needs someone to oversee the business, coordinate the work, provide direction to the people, and, ultimately, *get results*. If the work assigned to the leader's position could have been accomplished by only one person, instead of a team, the leader would not have been necessary. The organization would have needed only an individual contributor. If, on the other hand, the team was self-managed (rarely a good idea), the organization would not have needed someone to coordinate, direct, and oversee.

The expectation is that a team with a leader will be more productive and effective than either several individual contributors or a self-managed team. In order to capitalize on the benefits of a team over those of an individual, the leader must be willing to share and effectively distribute the workload. This sharing of work is an inevitable consequence of having more work than one person can do. A manager who does not delegate, or fails to delegate properly, stands to decrease an organization's productivity. The concept of *leadership leverage* is about multiplying the impact that a team, or organization, can have over what an individual alone is able to accomplish.

Delegating for Succession: Multiplying Your Impact

Another significant outcome of effective delegation is the development of subordinates, both for the positions they are currently in and for succession planning purposes. One of the impediments to growth is a paucity of people ready to take on larger responsibilities. Every function or team within a business should be seen as a petri dish for growing talent, with the manager as the scientist-in-charge! Regardless of one's feelings about Jack Welch's management style, one thing is clear about Welch—he made GE a talent generator. He was known for putting the burden of responsibility for developing people directly on the shoulders of their manager. It was not human resources (HR), not corporate, but management! In fact, part of GE managers' performance rating was determined by the rate and number of potential successors they were developing. Welch knew that the business would be able to optimize its market potential only when managers took up the mantle of growing their employees.

Selective and strategic delegation is a wonderful tool for accelerating the growth of a workforce. By giving stretch assignments, putting subordinates on critical business initiatives, and pushing subordinates to broaden their thinking and take risks, a manager can begin to test and expand the subordinates' capabilities. Research has consistently determined that on-the-job opportunities are the most instrumental means of developing leaders. These opportunities or stretch assignments, accompanied by mentoring and coaching, can greatly accelerate an individual's development. This acceleration will be well beyond what would normally take place by delegating randomly or on the basis of availability.

The Difficulty in Delegating: The Five Obstacles Holding You Back

The research is clear that when an organization is well managed, work is effectively distributed, and accountability is in place, productivity increases. A study by the Society for Human Resource Management found that the number one factor that negatively impacted productivity was poor management.[2] Given this research, why wouldn't leaders jump at the chance to capitalize on their teams through *leadership leverage?* We have identified five common reasons why leaders fail to delegate or delegate poorly.

- *Relationship management*: When a leader has risen from within an organization and is now the manager of people who were previously peers, the awkwardness of assigning responsibilities can hamper the early stages of their tenure. The irony of this discomfort is that the longer the new leader delays managing and delegating to previous peers, in an attempt to ease the transition, the more difficult it will become. A reestablishment of relationships, boundaries, and authority needs to come earlier rather than later in a leader's tenure.

- *Individualist outlook*: Individuals are promoted internally into leadership positions because of their exceptional work ethic, their creative solutions to difficult problems, their productivity, and, ultimately, their results. Their default pattern in times of stress or excessive workload is to do tasks themselves to ensure that they are done right. As a result, they often attempt to compensate for the inadequacies of their peers or the shortcomings in their work group. They can carry this pattern into management and leadership positions and, when work stacks up and deadlines loom, they work nights and weekends instead of distributing work.

- *Role adoption*: In a previous chapter, we discussed how new leaders in higher-level positions do not always appreciate the importance of focusing on the issues commensurate with their roles. An auto mechanic who is promoted to managing the garage will do better to think about pricing and attracting new customers than continuing to replace alternators. Effective delegation frees the leader to engage in more strategic areas of the company.

- *Context*: New leaders of an organization do not have the benefit of knowing the history of the business. In addition, they are just learning about those who report to them. They are wisely reluctant to delegate until they gain a better understanding of the situation. However, this reluctance often leads to a critical lack of delegation.

- *Process*: Particularly when a leader is a first-time manager, he or she may not have developed a personal process for delegating. A process would include a way for triaging work, matching delegated work to the right skill set, setting expectations, and having metrics in place for measuring progress toward task accomplishment. The lack of a process that can be applied universally to subordinates often inhibits the early manager from delegating work.

Those in leadership positions who do not understand the importance of delegating effectively will build weaker teams, slowdown decision-making, and, ultimately, become part of the reason for underachievement of their business. In addition, there is a built-in narcissism that some leaders must overcome. The "I-can-do-it-better-than-anyone-else" belief implies that the leader views himself or herself as the smartest, most capable person in their organization. Even if this is true, it will always be *more true* that a well-run group or team will beat the output of an individual. As *Start with Why* author Simon Sinek said, "A leader's job is not to do the work for others, it's to help others figure out how to do it themselves, to get things done, and to succeed beyond what they thought possible."[3] This is the essence of leadership.

Assessing the Team: A Prerequisite to Effective Delegation

The most pressing requirement for new leaders is to understand the *scope and scale* of their position. The next most important responsibility is to get to know and understand the capabilities of their subordinates. This is a prerequisite to assuring that the right talent is on in the team and that talent is deployed in ways that match skill set. If the deployment of talent on a team is not well determined, the new leader is delegating in a vacuum.

In addition, it is critical that leaders make their own judgments about the capabilities of people in their organizations. It is always prudent to assume that, when taking over a role previously occupied by someone else, there may have existed alliances, favorites, covert dyads, cliques, underutilized talent, and even shunned employees. All employees are likely to have had unique relationships with the previous manager. By simply taking someone else's word for the capabilities and performance of the team's talent, the new leader is effectively abdicating the most important aspect of the job—that of evaluating talent to maximize the joint capabilities of the team. Also, the charge of a new leader is almost always to take the business to the next level, not simply to maintain the status quo. This requires making a clear-eyed assessment of those in critical positions in the business.

Understanding Capabilities: A Cobbler or a Farrier

Shoes are shoes, right? But, capabilities required for one job may be vastly different for a job that may *seem* similar. Cobblers and farriers are both in the shoeing business, but mending shoes for a human is vastly different from shoeing a horse. A cobbler repairs shoes for people, but a farrier shoes horses—vastly different capabilities. By the same token, you want to be certain that you select just the right skill set for various tasks and not confuse what may seem to be similar proficiencies. In evaluating the capabilities of individuals, there are a few key questions that must be answered given a business's expectations. While some of these are obvious, some are subtler and nuanced. All need to be addressed prior to beginning delegation.

- *Emotional stability*: When evaluating an employee, it is always important to review how he or she had performed in the past as an indication of potential future behavior. Of course, behavior can change but there must be sufficient incentive for this to occur. Ask yourself questions such as: Is the subordinate reliable, consistent, and dependable? Can the subordinate be counted on to meet deadlines and work under pressure? In some cases, the capabilities of a diva or self-proclaimed star are so grand as to warrant putting up with their ups, downs, drama, and demanding nature. However, over time, their behaviors can be toxic.

- *Thinking capabilities*: Critical to delegating work is understanding the level of a subordinate's thinking and problem-solving skills. It is important to know if the individual is intellectually fluid and able to move easily from the tactical to the strategic, is highly detail oriented and more suited for analytic work, or more conceptual. Research by Dr. Anthony Gregorc developed a way to characterize learning styles.[4] Matching how individuals think with the demands of the job can optimize the performance of the subordinate, as illustrated in Figure 4.2.

- *Interpersonal competencies*: You need to understand how well developed an individual's interpersonal skills are regarding

Conceptual		
Strategic Flexible and fluid Learns through discussion Likes to brain storm Multiple interests	**Analytic** Structured and logical Prefers to work alone in quiet environment Likes to debate	
Creative and curious Dislikes structure Risk-taker Investigative Sees multiple solutions	Prefers order Precise/detailed Perfectionistic Practical/tactical Prefers step-by-step Values productivity	
Concrete		

Random (left side) / Systematic (right side)

Figure 4.2 Learning styles and assignments

behaviors such as being a team player; working well with others in solving problems; dealing effectively with conflict; and balancing listening with talking.

- *Work style*: Can the individual take on singular tasks that require working independently, either because the work is highly confidential or business-critical and cannot be shared? Is the individual a self-starter or does he or she need to be led and directed? Does the individual's effort vary upon the demands of others or is it always high, consistent, and self-directed?

- *Position match*: Does the skill set match the position? Is the individual in a position that aligns well with his or her capabilities and training? How broad is the individual's ability to learn new skills outside of his or her area of expertise? Is the person overqualified for the position, wanting more responsibility, and at-risk of leaving the organization? Or, is the person good at what he or she does and is content to keep doing it into the future?

Exploring these questions about subordinates is a critical first step in discerning whether or not a leader has the right people on their team in the right positions. Until the leader has a comfort level with the team and its capabilities and performance, it can be folly to delegate and expect consistent, high-level results.

Delegation Woes: Arriving at a Dead End

Imagine a leader who has reached a point when he or she understands, and is committed to, delegating as a means of maximizing productivity. This leader realizes that a high-functioning team can get more done than a high-functioning individual. This leader also understands the role effective delegation can play in the development of others for succession purposes. This leader has a process for understanding the capabilities of subordinates. Now, can you also imagine what might prevent that leader from becoming an effective delegator?

The Enemy in the Mirror: Getting Out of Our Own Way

Walt Kelly, creator of the long-running comic strip *Pogo*, created the first Earth Day poster that read, "We have met the enemy and he is us."[5] This humorous inscription is an accurate description of how individuals are often at the root of either perpetuating their own misery or standing between themselves and a good solution. This is clearly the case with effective delegation, which *always* begins with the personality of the leader. The more leaders have an awareness of their own personalities and tendencies, the better equipped they are to be effective in delegating to others. This includes understanding your temperament and your own work and leadership style.

The Hesitant Delegator

Whether it is to avoid conflict, because they are a perfectionist or because it is easier to "do it yourself," some managers undermine their leadership efforts by delegating only reluctantly. As a result, they take on all the work themselves and become bottlenecks making it impossible for work to get out in a timely manner. The great danger of "doing it yourself," is the long-term impact it has on subordinates. For the most part, employees want to make a contribution, be active, and grow in their positions. When they have either little to do, or the work they do have is perfunctory, they soon become disenchanted. Good employees leave and a leader is left with only underperformers. This then compounds problems when, or if, the leader finally does delegate work.

The Eager Delegator

At the other end of the spectrum is the manager who is only too ready to hand off work. These individuals, unbeknownst to management, have often risen in their organization on the backs of others. They are not discerning about what is delegated nor to whom it is given. These individuals lead on the basis of benign neglect, which they reframe as empowerment! It is often the case that their subordinates wonder what their manager is actually doing during work hours. Their good people, frequently overworked and underappreciated, leave. Like the hesitant delegator, the eager delegator is left with underperformers.

The Controlling Delegator

Some managers do delegate, but do not easily trust their subordinates and feel an exaggerated sense of pressure from their superiors. These are the ultimate pleasers who are always checking, and rechecking, to see how close their subordinates are to having their work completed or if they remember this detail or that detail. Once the subordinates complete their work, they can be assured that it will be scrutinized, revised, and possibly returned, complete with red marks. Controlling delegators really want to do the work themselves, but have learned that it is not possible; so they delegate but micromanage instead. It can be maddening to work for these managers, and good people do not work for them long!

You may have already guessed that all of these dysfunctional delegating styles are a result of insecurity. In the case of both the reluctant and the controlling delegator, they are fearful of being judged by their superiors. It becomes a self-fulfilling prophecy when their good people leave and both the volume and quality of work from their organizations decline. These dysfunctional delegators bring on themselves the very judgment they feared. Then they adopt the attitude of, "See, I told you so..." and intensify their reluctant or controlling habits.

In the case of the eager delegator, they become preoccupied with rising in the company and use the productivity of their group to justify their ambition. Often, when their teams are slaving away, these single-minded managers are actively promoting themselves to those in more powerful positions in the organization to try to gain their favor. What they fail to recognize is that their ambitious behavior is more transparent than they realize. Their insecurities have manifested in ways that ultimately repel, rather than attract, their superiors and their subordinates!

Case Study

The Operation Was Successful But the Company Died

The founder of a small, but growing, auto insurance company was frustrated with the inability of his business to develop beyond its current level. The company seemed to have significant opportunity and very capable staff but, once it had reached a critical mass of business, it seemed impossible to get to the next level. The founder contracted with us to investigate and help him determine what could be done to ameliorate the situation. We conducted an in-depth organizational analysis through multiple employee interviews. It did not take long for the answer to become undeniably clear.

The company's inability to grow further was primarily because the founder insisted on being involved in every decision, even those that could easily be made at a lower level. We recommended that the founder hire a president to run the day-to-day business so that the founder could do what he did best, business development. After a brief search, a suitable candidate was found and became the new president. Within three months, we received a distress call from the new president who said that the founder would not let him run the business. The founder had a daily list of things that he expected the president to attend, which rapidly undermined any authority of the position and usurped the time needed for the president to complete his own agenda. Knowing the founder expected it, employees continued to go to the founder for direction instead of going to the new president. Within six months, the new president resigned believing that the founder was unwilling to delegate the responsibilities that would have freed the founder's time to do what was necessary for the company to thrive. Within a year, many of the employees had left the company unable to envision a career path in what had become a failing business.

The commitment to wisely delegate duties, in order to focus on greater growth, is often a founder's dilemma. In this case, the founder's inability to make that wise commitment to delegate appropriate duties resulted in the demise of his business.

Delegation Wins: Arriving Exactly Where You Intended

Sustaining high-level production from a function or a business requires a manager to truly become a leader and delegate from a position of confidence, rather than one of insecurity. This means that leaders need to have a broader understanding of their roles in the context of their businesses. They understand the importance of their organization delivering high-quality and timely products or services in a collaborative, noncompetitive, manner. They put the needs of the organization above their own ambitions. They see the delegation of work as an opportunity to develop those under them. They understand the need to match skill sets with tasks. They have methods to track what they have delegated to ensure that work does not fall between the cracks as a result of their own multiple work demands. They will become known as the leaders whom others strive to emulate and for whom others want to work.

Establishing a Process: Getting Results While Staying Involved

Leaders who have developed an effective delegation style are thoughtful and intentional in the allocation of duties and the assignment of levels of authority. They may be interpersonally engaging, but are typically demanding in a way that brings out the best in others. They have high expectations for themselves and for those in their organizations. Their delegation is typified by process management.

Process Management

Good leaders establish a process for the delegation of major items. They know that, without a process in place, the ability to track the progress of an initiative is difficult and the ability to track multiple initiatives is impossible. Processes include:

- *Clear expectations*: Making sure that outcomes are clear in terms of the quality of outcome and quantity of work to be done.
- *Ownership*: Someone must be ultimately responsible for the oversight, quality, and timeliness of a project. This cannot be delegated to a committee and needs to be considered a major part of the focus of only *one* individual. Periodically, two or more individuals will volunteer to take ownership, but never let this happen. *An initiative with more than one owner ultimately has no owner!* This ownership must be given with trust and power and the assurance that the leader will not be looking over his or her subordinate's shoulder during the process.
- *Timelines*: Monitoring closely the progress of an initiative on a timeline schedule is a critical piece to any initiative review. This assumes that a schedule has been created and reviewed prior to commencing the work.
- *Status updates*: Coding the status of an initiative (on schedule, slightly behind, way behind) is very important. This gives the owner of the initiative a sense of where attention or additional resources need to be given.
- *Communication*: How, when, how often, by whom, and to whom updates will be provided all need to be clearly specified. Communications need to be tied to subsequent work assignments to further the initiative.
- *Consequences and rewards*: Some initiatives are of such a scale or are so critical that their success or failure is tied to financial benefits to the imitative team or owner.

While it is crucial to have a good process for doing work, it is not enough. The process must be paired with quantifiable metrics. Others (customers, superiors, and regulators) are expecting the work to be completed in a manner that is of the highest quality. Effective leaders know that *what gets measured gets done*. Metrics identify where a project stands with regard to resource utilization (e.g., manpower, financials) against where it was predicted to be. The elements of metrics are quality, quantity, timeliness, and resource utilization. The metrics of an initiative are always the criteria for accountability.

Work, Work Everywhere: Differentiating and Triaging

Our experience with leaders *at all levels* is that they frequently do not differentiate well between what they accept to take on or what they choose to delegate. When it comes to incoming requests it is not uncommon for leaders to be invited to multiple meetings, encouraged to become members of several committees or task forces, and included on numerous e-mails that do not directly involve them or their organization. These demands can be irrelevant and overwhelming. A critical early-term behavior is setting clear boundaries and determining those requests (most of them) that the leader should decline. Most companies are out of control with the number of meetings, e-mails, and useless information that is passed around as important. Most of this information is neither urgent nor important. The undiscerning leader may think that he or she is being conscientious in responding to as many of these requests as he or she is able to. Overly ambitious people may perceive attendance at multiple meetings as an avenue person to "see and be seen."

As mature, secure leaders begin to grasp the importance of their role, and the business or organization they oversee, they realize the importance of becoming more discerning in what they take on. A good first step is to ask why an item or initiative is being assigned to them and how it aligns to the charter of their organization. Deciding what *not* to do or accept is as important as deciding what you do accept. This process is crucial in making sure the work of your organization gets completed.

In order to define their workload, leaders must have a method for characterizing work. It is important for leaders to have a process to determine: what work they can or should do; what work should be delegated; and what work is not worthy of being done at all. The following categories provide a guideline for making these determinations:

- *Aligned/critical*: The work clearly supports the charge of the organization and is important to the overall success of the business. Plan it.

- *Aligned/low critical*: While the work may fall within the
  purview of the organization, it is not currently critical to the
  success of the organization. Make it a lower priority.
- *Misaligned*: The work is either not aligned with the purpose
  of the organization or is unrelated to the overall success of the
  business. Dump it.

Once you have decided the work that should be taken on by your team, a secondary sorting will help to delegate the work to the right people with the right skill sets. Determine which level or role in the organization the work is best suited to. This helps determine who should be involved. Keep in mind that the higher up the role in the organization, the more the individual should focus on strategic issues. It is also important to determine if the work would be a good opportunity for an individual to grow and develop.

Likewise, sort your work for delegation by complexity. More complex, strategic, and multifaceted work should go to your most capable subordinates, not necessarily your most tenured. In fact, you need to have enough steady, stable individuals in your organization to undertake routine work. Figure 4.3 can help you determine to whom you should delegate work once you have conducted the second sorting.

Delegation matrix		
Work difficulty / Complex	Delegate for growth	Delegate critical and difficult
Work difficulty / Simple	Delegate simple or routine	Do not delegate
	Adequate or newer/Hi potentials	**Strong, well developed**
	Strength of skillset	

Figure 4.3 Delegation matrix

A note on volume: The determination for how much an individual can take on at a time rests on the shoulders of the individual, not the manager. The individual and manager must have an initial discussion that makes it clear that the individual needs to speak up when his or her "plate is full." Managers should not, and cannot, determine when one of their subordinates has all he or she is able to work on at a time. Also, this can become a point of development for the subordinate answering questions about capacity, assertiveness, and ability to manage multiple projects at a time.

Sorry, Here Is What You Can Never Delegate

Even with the most capable leaders who delegate effectively, trust their subordinates, and have well-developed processes, there will always be some work that can be done only by the leader. This work cannot be delegated, even to the most trusted, competent subordinates. The leader has no choice but to do the work on his or her own. This work typically falls into one of these categories.

- *Confidential*: It is often the case that a business is involved in activities that must be closely held for competitive or legal purposes. This would include issues pertaining to mergers and acquisitions; lawsuits; personnel matters; downsizing, and similar issues.
- *Business critical*: Often, there will be work that a leader's superior has requested in which only the leader can be involved. The matter is not confidential, but is of such importance that no one else can see it through.
- *Resource constraints*: There will be times that there are so many demanding issues that all resources are full to capacity. Good leaders know there are times when they will have to do work that is "beneath their pay grade," when no one else is available.
- *Emergencies*: Businesses periodically have "all-hands-on-deck" problems when everyone must dig in. This relates to urgent customer problems or opportunities and are not optional.
- *Customer requests*: Developing great customer relationships can have a downside, in that there are certain customers who

will not want anyone but their contact to do work for them. In fact, some customers will threaten to leave unless they can keep the relationship they have developed and trusted, leaving little choice in the matter.

At times, there will be other issues to which the leader, and only the leader, can attend. However, *these must be the exception and not the rule.* The leader needs to avoid falling back into the trap of doing it alone and failing to strategically delegate. Leaders must keep in mind how to *leverage* the work of their employees and not do the work themselves. Maintaining the discipline of effective delegation is critical to the success of a leader, the leader's subordinates, and the business.

Coach's Corner

Effective delegation is one of the paramount responsibilities of a successful leader. Increased productivity, employee satisfaction, and even succession planning all follow from proper delegation. This type of quality *leadership leverage* can be the rising tides that lift all boats and, ultimately, the metric through which a leader is judged. After all, it is the success of the team that a leader is tasked with at the end of the day.

Four Tips for Effective Delegation

1. **Determine What Work Should Be Delegated**
   - Triage incoming work to determine what ought to be tackled by your team and what is not of core importance. Further divide the work of your team between what only you can do and what you are able to delegate.
2. **Fit the Work to the Employee**
   - Tailor the work you delegate to your employees' skill sets and temperaments. Assign complex, multifaceted work to those suited for it. Send routine work to your stable and steady types.
3. **Delegate for Development**
   - Give "stretch assignments" to train employees on the job to use greater layers of sophistication and prepare key employees within the organization for greater responsibility.

Chapter 4 Survey

Effective delegation	Much too little		Barely too little		Just right	Barely too much		Much too much	
Please insert an "X" in the appropriate box to indicate your answer	−4	−3	−2	−1	0	+1	+2	+3	+4
How often do you determine what parts of your workload ought to be delegated?									
How often do you consider a subordinate's skills when delegating responsibilities to him or her?									
How often do you triage your work to determine what is of core importance?									

4. **Have a Process**
   - Pair the tasks you delegate with precise timelines, status updates, and communication so that expectations are clear. Give your employees ownership of their projects and determine specific intended outcomes.

Areas for Development

As you think about your company, what are the top three ways you can better leverage your employees through delegation?

1. _____

2. _____

3. _____

Notes

1. Cherkasky (2016).
2. *Workplace Productivity* (A Study by the Society of Human Resource Management, 2005).
3. Sinek (2009).
4. Gregorc (2004).
5. *"We have met the enemy and he is us."* http://thisdayinquotes.com/2011/04/we-have-met-enemy-and-he-is-us.html (accessed December 13, 2016).

References

"We have met the enemy and he is us." http://thisdayinquotes.com/2011/04/we-have-met-enemy-and-he-is-us.html (accessed December 13, 2016).

Cherkasky, S. 2016. "How to Delegate for Improved Productivity." *Change Management Consulting.* http://www.cmc-changemanagement.com/infocenter/Downloads/Delegate_for_Productivity.pdf (accessed December 13, 2016).

Gregorc, A.F. 2004. *The Gregorc Style Delineator.* AFG Books.

Sinek, S. 2009. *Start with Why.* New York: Penguin Books.

Workplace Productivity (A Study by the Society of Human Resource Management, 2005).

CHAPTER 5

Difficult Conversations: Business Issues and Performance Discussions

Conflict as Opportunity: The Mantle of Leadership

Walking across the airport toward his departure gate, a man spots a familiar person out of the corner of his eye. On the other side of the large concourse, he sees his company's vice president of human resources (HR). He changes course to greet the vice president when he is stopped in his tracks. A woman is sitting next to the vice president. She is a direct report to him, and they are being affectionate with each other in ways reserved for lovers. Not only are they both married to other people, but the vice president had recently hired the woman and moved her across the country to work in his office. The observer immediately feels a knot in the pit of his stomach and quickly walks away unseen. Not only is he shocked, but he wonders what he should do about what he has just seen. The vice president outranks him in the company and works in a different business function altogether. What to do? What to do?

The sales director of a regional, privately held technology company has been told by the regional president, his boss, that the region has had a banner year. As a result, bonuses for the region are assured and the region has made its contribution to the internal employee stock plan. In fact, the president says that the year's revenues were so good that he was going to squirrel away several million dollars in still unreported revenue to go against next year's budget. The president winks and adds that this will ensure that the following year will also be a good year. The sales director makes a grimacing grin and walks away. The sales director knows that, while this is technically legal, it is unethical. It has the effect of underreporting revenues and internal stock will be priced lower than it should be, potentially hurting retiring employees waiting for year-end results before selling their shares. The sales director becomes both anxious and perplexed, torn between what he should do, what he can do, and the consequences of both.

The operations manager of a manufacturing plant is known to have a harsh and direct style. This has generally been tolerated by her staff and rarely reached the level of requiring serious attention. However, recently, it has been noticed by several of her staff that her abrasive style has become inflamed to the point of bordering on being abusive. As a result, the staff is beginning to talk to each other about requesting transfers or quitting altogether. The manager's behavior has created a vicious cycle in which her abrasiveness diminishes motivation and productivity which serves to further heighten her tone perpetuating the downward cycle. Her peers and her boss either do not recognize her behavior or are determined not to address it. Her direct reports are wondering what could be done to address her behavior and, in all sincerity, how they could help their manager regain her footing.

Situations like these occur regularly in business settings. Most day-to-day issues that arise are not elevated to the level of legal violations. Many demonstrate primarily ineffective leadership style; interpersonal conflicts and differences; white lies to cover for some performance deficits; or taking shortcuts that do not conform to company policy. At times, these issues broaden to include behaviors and consequences originating from *outside* of their organizations.

Moving into a leadership role is more than a promotion: *it is a responsibility*. The higher up individuals ascend in an organization, the more responsibility they have for the consequences of the behaviors of those in their organizations. Holding others accountable often requires leaders to have difficult conversations. Our experience is that many, if not most, individuals shy away from having direct, constructive discourse about difficult situations. However, without having difficult conversations about important issues, nothing will change. In this chapter, we will lay out a framework for how leaders need to think about, address, and effectively deal with conflict and how to hold themselves and others accountable.

All of the aforementioned examples are actual ones that have occurred in companies with which we have worked. In the first example, the individual who observed the vice president of HR in a compromising relationship determined that he could not go through typical HR channels to report the incident. Instead, he called the company ethics hotline that was managed by the corporate legal department, which then looked into the situation. Ultimately, the vice president of HR was terminated for misappropriation of company funds because the expenses for his dalliance were charged on the company credit card. In the second example, the sales director reported the incident to the chief financial officer (CFO). The outcome of the investigation was that the regional president was demoted, put on probation, had his bonus taken away, and was required to attend an ethics course on fiduciary responsibility. In the final example, the direct reports of the abrasive operations manager scheduled an intervention in a formal meeting. The direct reports outlined their concerns and offered support to carry some of the load of the operations manager that could diminish her frustration. They also warned that, if these problems persisted in the future, they would be forced to go to HR to report them. All of these cases required action on the part of the employees, and not simply observation. We will look at the best way to approach escalating business issues and performance discussions.

Escalating Business Issues: Weighing Risk

The range of problems that require discussion in an organization varies from those that are business critical to those that are simple nuisances. When thinking of raising potentially volatile issues to more senior leaders, a few guidelines can help in deciding whether or not to take the risk and how to go about doing so. The seriousness of an issue determines the need and timing for surfacing it. At the more routine end of the continuum are the identification of suboptimal or legacy processes, services or products, unreported employee performance, and minor safety and health issues. More pronounced issues are violations of company policy, legal or regulatory violations, and fraud.

A technology firm with which we consult had an officer who was also the owner of several local food trucks. This was not a problem until another of the company's employees went to one of these food trucks for lunch and happened to see this officer working during a time that he was supposed to be conducting company business! The company employee debated whether or not to raise the issue to management. Did he have the right or the authority to raise it? If it was simply a one-time error in judgment, would he look petty by escalating it? If he did report it, to whom would he do so? HR? Legal? Management? Finally, he did decide to raise the issue and, after further investigation, the company officer was terminated.

Clearly, a leader cannot, and should not, address every issue that arises because there are typically too many for them to effectively address. Like any other matter, leaders need to discern those issues that require attention and those that can be allowed to slide. We call this the continuum of accountability (see Figure 5.1.) At the lower end of the continuum are issues that are mere annoyances and can be let go. At the upper end of the continuum are issues that must be addressed quickly because they present significant financial, legal, or regulatory risk to the company. It is important for a leader to assess the degree of risk in a given situation to determine the necessity and timing of addressing the issue at hand.

Minor Annoyances

These include processes that no longer make sense but are not overly damaging to the business, and as such likely do not merit escalation. They are often held onto by employees who may have a vested interest in keeping things the way they are. In one of our client companies, the head of sales

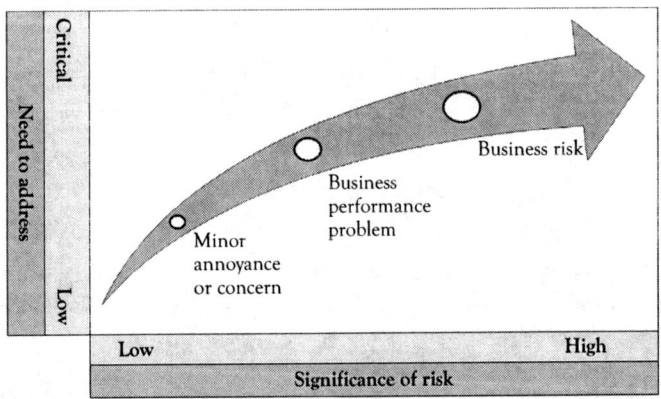

Figure 5.1 The continuum of accountability

insists on entering monthly charges to customers manually on a spreadsheet when a much quicker, and more accurate, technical solution exists. This company officer has been extremely successful in generating business year-over-year. He has been with the company for many years and feels the need to control the input of information rather than allow others to do it much more quickly and reliably. While it is an annoyance to those in finance and bookkeeping, it is not a major risk to the company. They have resigned themselves to leaving it that way until he retires, at which time they can transition this work to more modern methods.

Business Performance

There are often practices that impact business performance but are neither illegal nor a violation of regulatory or compliance statutes. Such issues should be escalated only if they are of high impact to the company. Examples would include:

- Using suppliers because of their relationships with management, even though they are more expensive and do not provide greater quality than other potential suppliers
- Maintaining a poor-performing employee because he or she has a friendship or long-time relationship with someone in senior management
- Nepotism or cronyism in the hiring process (when it does not violate company policy)
- Using materials that meet minimum federal or state requirements but are not of a high quality for the consumer
- Excessive breakage of inventory due to weakness in the quality control process

Business Risk

When an issue surfaces that may put the business at risk, it is clearly worthy of being elevated to the right internal authorities. These issues would include items such as fraud, regulatory and compliance violations, health and safety vulnerabilities, workplace inappropriateness (hostile work environment, sexual harassment, bullying), product problems, and kickbacks. There are numerous examples of companies skirting federal regulations in an attempt to cut costs and accelerate sales. When leaders identify illegal practices within their companies, they have an ethical responsibility to reveal them. These issues are dichotomous in nature; they are black or white, right or wrong. There is little gray area. To know they exist and *not* reveal them amounts to complicity.

"I suppose I'll be the one to mention the elephant in the room."

Figure 5.2 The elephant in the room

Source: andrewgenn/Depositphotos.com. http://depositphotos.com/60466579/stock-illustration-elephant-in-the-room.html (accessed January 14, 2017).

Bill Bado, a former Wells Fargo banker in Pennsylvania, refused to open phony bank and credit accounts as instructed by his branch manager. Instead, he called the Wells Fargo ethics hotline and sent an e-mail to HR in 2013, flagging unethical sales activities that he was being instructed to conduct. Eight days after he sent the e-mail, he was terminated. The reason given was tardiness. However, in September of 2016, Wells Fargo admitted to firing 5,300 employees for engaging in these same shocking tactics and paid $185 million in penalties. Although he disavowed knowledge in an attempt to let lower-level people take the hit, Wells Fargo chief executive officer (CEO) John Stumpf subsequently had to resign. Apparently, Stumpf believed that the *buck stops in the middle*! Other brave Wells Fargo employees came forward later, indicating they had also complained and met a fate similar to Bado's.[1] While the Whistleblower Protection Act of 1989 and the Whistleblower Protection Enhancement Act of 2012 were created to prevent retaliation for whistleblowers, there still exist penalties for voicing difficult issues to management as well as fear of reprisal.

Leaders at all levels in a company have opportunities to demonstrate their commitment to leadership, mostly when they are faced with taking unpopular stands. The heroes in business are those who, like Bill Bado, recognize problems in their companies and are willing to reveal them, risking what may be career-limiting consequences. While most issues of concern do not rise to the level of the recent Wells Fargo fraud, there are routinely issues that arise in business that are the *elephants in the room.* Everyone knows they exist but few have the courage to speak up and address them.

Considering the Reality of Change

For issues that are of low impact to a business, leaders need to be realistic about the probability of change arising as a result of their raising the issue. There are some issues that are simply not worth the time and effort required to escalate because the likelihood of change is low. An example of this would be exposing a friend of the boss (FOB) who is a sluggard in the organization. Raising the issue would likely not change the situation and may even irritate the boss. Is the cost worth the unlikely benefit?

Looking in the Mirror: Weighing the Costs

Choices that leaders make transpire in the context of their position in their organization. Many choices are accompanied by the possibility of being promoted, encouraged, passed over, or fired. The tension of these various possibilities infuses decisions with the fear, pride, and ambition that accompanies these changes in fortune. The higher the stakes of a scenario, the more these emotions come into play.

Prior to revealing a difficult issue, leaders need to pause and consider whether or not doing so is wise. Once a contentious issue is revealed, there is often no going back. There are several matters of personal motivation that leaders must consider prior to elevating an issue:

- Being aware of the extent to which raising issues are done to further their own careers
- Considering when a bad history exists between them and other employees that may be negatively effected by the raising of an issue
- Having a clear understanding of their personal values and how they interact with the values of the business before taking action
- Asking if a fear of potential consequences is restraining them from taking action

There are scenarios when it is right and necessary to elevate business issues and neglecting to raise them when individuals and the company are at great risk is even more detrimental. By considering these criteria *prior* to raising an issue, leaders can ensure that their motives are free of personal agenda and they will only raise issues that have a high likelihood of change or have high value in being escalated and potentially resolved.

Case Study

Preparing for "The Talk"

A large nonprofit organization that focuses on community health had appointed a new managing director while the founder stayed on as CEO. The new managing director was hired to be responsible for all day-to-day operations. After six months in her new position, the managing director called us to discuss ongoing issues with the founder that interfered with her ability to effectively manage day-to-day operations. The founder, a local celebrity and icon in the community, was having difficulty staying out of the details of the business. One health fair found him trimming the ribbons on a company diorama, and side coaching hourly employees. He was also frequently making additional commitments for the new managing director and her staff without informing them, much less getting their consent. The managing director, knowing that we had a previous relationship with the founder, appealed to us to subtly deliver messages to the founder to help him better understand the boundaries of his new position as CEO. We believed that this approach was fraught with several ethical and logistical conundrums that made it impossible for us to accept the assignment. We told the managing director that we could either refer her to another consultant or provide her with a framework for raising difficult issues with the CEO (or anyone else). She asked us for the framework. We gave her guidelines for clarifying the issues at hand, as well as crafting and preparing the message she wanted to deliver, including rehearsing with a qualified confidant. We also recommended ongoing processes for follow-up and fine-tuning

(Continued)

role differentiators. The managing director took our counsel and followed up with us in four months to let us know that she had followed our framework to have discussions with the CEO about her concerns. She said that both she and the CEO had become more comfortable and effective in their roles. They had also set up ongoing "check-in" meetings to continue to refine roles, clarify responsibilities, and manage their communication.

Raising an Issue: The Mechanics of Escalation

Once leaders are clear about the issue they want to escalate and are committed to escalating it, their message needs to be delivered in a thoughtful and intentional manner. It may be better not to raise an issue at all than to raise it in a way that's ineffective. The following three steps will set you on the path to a successful escalation.

Crafting the Message

Taking time to carefully craft the initial communication regarding an issue will ensure that the message you want to deliver is the message that is received. It is important that the message is concise, hits your main points, and serves as a headline. The more data points a leader has to substantiate the message, the more powerful and credible the message will be. To have the greatest impact, make the key points the ones that signify the major infractions.

Preparing for Delivery

It is often helpful to have another qualified professional as a sounding board to get feedback on both content and intended approach. However, it is also important to avoid *triangulation* (involving those who are not part of the problem and cannot possibly help in the solution). It ultimately contributes to the creation of a toxic environment. A qualified confidant, with no investment in the situation and the willingness to challenge your thinking, can help clarify the issue, sharpen main points, and assist with methods of delivery. The confidant can also be used to rehearse key messages and anticipate questions or challenges.

Selecting the Recipient

Identifying the initial recipient of the message is critical. It is imperative to escalate issues only to those who are likely to take some kind of action. It is common in organizations for employees to raise issues only to never hear about them again. The issues raised may end up joining multiple other concerns previously raised in the company's issue graveyard. Also, only deliver the issue to those who also have the authority, courage, fortitude, and relationships in the organization to deal with the issue.

Delivering for Impact

To maximize impact, make a formal appointment, arrive with a clear agenda, state your case as rehearsed, and listen to any responses and questions. Discuss the issue directly, clearly, and openly. Because there is no hidden agenda, delivery can be unguarded and with a problem-solving tone. Ask what follow-up is necessary and when you can expect an update regarding the status of the resolution of the issue. Document the meeting for future reference.

Once these steps are completed, the leader has demonstrated the courage to raise the issue, the discipline to prepare for its delivery, and the determination to convey the difficult issue to the proper authorities. The leader has become part of the solution and has not perpetuated the problem. At this point, what is left is waiting for updates and recognizing the limits of personal responsibility and authority. The ultimate disposition of the issue rests in the hands of final decision-makers. Job well done!

A Special Note on Performance Discussions: Moving from Discipline to Growth

Of all the difficult conversations to have, performance-related conversations rank among those that leaders fret over most. Our experience is that most leaders fail, or suboptimize, opportunities to address performance issues. Most would rather walk on hot coals than to have discussions with individuals about their poor performance and productivity. While underperformance can become business critical, it typically impairs productivity of the individual and, sometimes, the productivity of others when the individual creates a bottleneck in a process. We have identified the three types of managers who ineffectively approach performance discussions.

The Shirker

These managers are poor communicators to the point that they do not have performance discussions at all! They often rationalize that "things will work themselves out over time," or that their employees "know what to do" in order to change without further explanation. They do not have difficult discussions with either their employees or others in the organization, or they procrastinate to the extent that the original issue either resolves itself or escalates to a higher level. These managers are characterized by assuming that their employees can "read their minds." They are often in denial of difficult issues and seem oblivious that some behaviors or performance issues need their attention. They are usually ineffective and are neither liked nor respected.

The Pleaser

This is the most common performance discussion behavior we encounter. These leaders have the mistaken belief that by having difficult discussions they will negatively impact their working relationships. In effect, by using their fear of consequences as a justification for inaction, they fail to address problems effectively. This inaction then serves, inadvertently, to reinforce the bad behavior of their employees. When they finally do have a performance discussion, they have it too late, too tentatively, or too indirectly. After leaving the discussion, the employee may still not have a clear sense that he or she needs to change his or her behavior! Then, when such employees are ultimately put on a performance plan or are terminated, they are in shock because they believe they were not given sufficient warning about their poor performance. Pleaser managers fear openness and boldness, seeing these behaviors as insensitive or damaging.

Because they are liked, their teams will often cover for them, but this vicious cycle can only last so long. Pleaser managers may be liked but are not respected.

The Bruiser

Interestingly, the same discomfort resident in the shirker is apparent in a vastly different way in the bruiser. Bruisers also dislike these discussions (unless they are psychopathic) and they use a hit-and-run approach to performance discussions. In such meetings, they have a one-way discussion during which they tell the employee all that he or she is doing wrong. They have these discussions in a shaming manner that is brusque and may border on being abusive.

These abrasive communicators take pride in having had the discussion but are no more tied to the results than the shirker. The focus is not one of problem-solving but one of intimidation and threats. The employee leaves the meeting disheartened, demoralized, and fearful. Bruising managers are fearful too, primarily fearing vulnerability. They mistakenly equate vulnerability with weakness. These kinds of managers are feared but not respected.

"Your evaluation is based on the next 30 seconds. Go!"

Figure 5.3 The performance review

Source: andrewgenn/Depositphotos.com. http://depositphotos.com/62763019/stock-illustration-evaluation-is-happening.html (accessed January 14, 2017).

Performance Discussions Done Correctly

To become effective at having successful performance discussions, leaders must have a positive framework in which to engage the employee. When performance discussions are seen as win-lose fights between two opposing points of view, they are more likely to result in outcomes in which all parties lose. However, when leaders begin with the assumption of *positive intent* and the belief that most people want to do their best, approaching the discussion takes on a much different outlook. Approaching performance discussions with more of a problem-solving than a discipline-metering approach creates a better emotional environment for potential success. We have identified a six-stage process to having effective performance discussions.

1. **Identifying patterns**: We operate on the basis of "the rule of three." If a behavior occurs (or does not occur) once, it is simply an incident. If the same behavior occurs twice, it could be a coincidence. However, the third occurrence of the same behavior demonstrates a clear pattern and time to act. The main objective is for the manager to be able to clearly recognize a pattern of employee behavior in which the performance of the employee is diminished. Once this pattern is recognized, it is time to act. Having data to support the discussion is a prerequisite to having the discussion. We should add that there are occasionally situations that are clearly so critical that the occurrence of them happening once is enough to take action.

2. **Understanding root causes**: While there are times when diminished performance is due to employees being lazy, devious, and deceptive, these situations are usually the exception. Far more often, when a previously high-performing employee demonstrates diminished or impaired behavior, it is likely that there are other factors at work. It is important for the manager to understand the root causes of declining performance so that they are addressed and the manager is not guilty of "symptom chasing." Among the potential root causes of declining performance are:

   • *Unclear expectations*: It is often the case that a manager has not been clear about expectations for an assignment or role. It is interesting that this lack of clarity of expectations is prevalent at both ends of the management tenure continuum. Newer managers and leaders who have not had the experience of managing and delegating often fail to set expectations appropriately. It is also true that highly tenured leaders may take for granted that the work assigned is already well understood and needs no clarification. Both overlook the basics of delegation (see Chapter 4).

● Overqualification: Sometimes, individuals have more experience and knowledge than their position requires and may be bored and on auto-pilot. In these cases, they may inadvertently overlook details required for routine work, but are capable and willing to take on greater challenges. They may be an underused resource waiting to be discovered!

● Lacking resources: Not having the right resources to success-fully complete a project can hamper results.

● Underqualification: During a robust economy with low unemployment, individuals are often promoted quickly and given greater responsibilities without adequate preparation. It is possible that they could be prepared with more education and training. It is also possible that they are simply not capa-ble of handling the position or the responsibilities to which they have been assigned.

● Personal problems: Issues outside of work often impact performance at work. While it is difficult to address these issues sensitively and carefully, some employees genuinely need to be cut some slack temporarily when their personal lives severely collide with their work lives. Showing support during such times can endear employees to a leader and can increase loyalty and productivity once personal issues subside.

It is critical that the leader spend adequate pre-discussion time understanding root causes so that the best performance meeting out-come can occur.

3. **Visualizing a positive outcome:** Once root causes are understood, leaders need to consider ahead of the performance meeting what the best outcome would be. While the interaction during the meeting may change the outcome, by visualizing and mentally rehearsing what a good outcome would look like, leaders are able to shape the meeting in a more positive direction.

4. **Creating a problem-solving environment**: When leaders enter into performance discussions with the stated intent of trying to solve a problem, rather than to discipline, intimidate, or shame an employee, everyone's anxiety level decreases significantly, raising the possibility of finding solutions. Shifting the discussion to one in which the leader has a sincere interest in the growth and development of the employee gives the employee a second chance to succeed. Who among us does not periodically need a do-over!

5. **Developing a plan**: Imperative to helping an employee return to, regain, or attain a level of performance that is acceptable requires the creation of a clear improvement plan. This is done in a manner in which the manager offers whatever assistance necessary. Successful plans have tangible, measurable targets and realistic time frames.

6. **Following up**: Our experience is that, often, even good leaders fail to follow up and have regular updates with their employees, following such discussions. Very little benefit is yielded when no follow-up plan is created and implemented to measure improvement. At the end of any performance discussion, the leader and employee must put regular meetings on the calendar and adhere to them. During these meetings employees provide updates on their improvement plan.

Even when a leader has followed the aforementioned process, performance issues may persist. It is imperative that the leader take stronger actions to remedy such situations. Leaders can take this stronger action knowing that they have made patient efforts to solve problems in a constructive manner.

Coach's Corner

Difficult discussions must be had in any organization. When organizational or personnel issues arise, a leader must determine how to bring them up and who to bring them up to (if they need to be brought up at all.) The best leaders prepare for difficult discussions so that they can speak honestly and confidently to those in their organizations.

Four Tips for Navigating Difficult Discussions

1. **Deciding When to Speak Up**
   - Before elevating a business issue to your superiors determine both the severity and impact of the issue. If the danger it poses is business critical or high impact, bring it up to the proper authority. If not, proceed with caution.

2. **Practice Your Speech**
   - Before raising a business issue craft your message so that your main point is clear, and identify the best audience for your message. Practice your delivery with a close and qualified confidant until you are ready.

3. **Deciding When Not to Speak Up**
   - If there is little chance that a business issue will be resolved, or if you may have ulterior motives for raising it, it may be best not to raise the issue.

4. **Approaching Performance Discussions**
   - Frame performance discussions as opportunities for growth. Finding ways to explain poor performance that do not make the employee defensive will help reduce discomfort and lead to a successful shift in behavior.

Areas for Development

As you think about issues you face in your company, what are the top three ways you can address them more effectively?

1. _____

2. _____

3. _____

Chapter 5 Survey

Difficult conversations	Much too little	Barely too little	Just right	Barely too much	Much too much
Please insert an "X" in the appropriate box to indicate your answer	−4	−3	−2	−1	0	+1	+2	+3	+4
How often do you broach difficult issues at work?									
How much time do you spend preparing for difficult discussions?									
How often do you take time to frame difficult discussions in a positive light?									

Note

1. Egan (2016).

Reference

Egan, M. 2016. "I called Wells Fargo hotline and was fired." *CNNMoney*, September 21. *http://money.cnn.com/2016/09/21/investing/ wells-fargo-fired-workers-retaliation-fake-accounts/*

CHAPTER 6

The Talent Expedition

The vast amount of business executives who unexpectedly fail gives an indication of the difficulty of selecting and promoting the best individuals into greater roles of responsibility. Recent failures include:

- McDonald's chief executive officer (CEO) Don Thompson, a 25-year employee, left in January 2015 as a result of declining sales.
- Yishan Wong, recruited to be Reddit's CEO in 2011, resigned in 2014, less than three years in the position, citing extreme job stress.
- Mattel CEO Bryan Stockton was terminated without cause in January 2015, as global sales fell 7 percent. He had been with Mattel for 15 years.
- Scott Thompson was recruited from PayPal to be the CEO of Yahoo in January 2012. Yahoo abruptly terminated him in May 2012 in part for having misrepresented his college degree.

These examples highlight the most visible and confounding aspect of business—the successful hiring, developing, and deploying of people. When executives fail after having been successful in their companies for years (Don Thompson and Bryan Stockton), or successful in other companies (Yishan Wong and Scott Thompson), it demonstrates the difficulty of both promoting and hiring individuals to leadership roles. While these examples are of CEOs, it happens at every level in organizations.

There is no greater challenge that leaders face than employing the highest level of talent possible in their organizations. In this chapter, we will review common pitfalls that leaders face in identifying and hiring talent. We will also present some guidelines for leaders to consider when they have the opportunity to bring new talent into their organizations. These guidelines apply to both internal promotions and external hires.

It has become a cliché that when CEOs announce their company's quarterly results they open with comments depicting their people as the most important aspect of their businesses. However, the time these CEOs spend on executive development, mentoring, and consulting with employees pales when compared to the time spent on their products, services, customers, processes, markets, and financials. This is not to say that such executives are exaggerating or intentionally ignoring their people. Rather it is that the people end of a business is more difficult and complex than the technical aspects of a business. As Heinz von Foerster, scientist and creator of parallel computing, observed, "hard sciences are successful because they deal with the soft problems; soft sciences are struggling because they deal with the hard problems."[1]

It is no wonder that much of the work invested in succession planning and talent development ultimately comes to naught. Such noble attempts include creating development plans, establishing internal "universities," and investing millions of dollars in employee software management. Human performance, motivation, and behaviors are particularly difficult to predict. They are typically not able to be quantified in a manner that ensures accurate forecasting.

In this chapter, we will look at the Do's and Don'ts of hiring. If you work at an executive search firm or human resources department you may want to beware! We make a couple of controversial conclusions you may not like. Nevertheless, we have found them to be true.

Promote from Within or Hire Externally

Is it best to promote internally or hire externally? The two different approaches are respectively referred to by companies as *build or buy* strategies. There are pros and cons to both considerations. In some cases, it is an easy decision. When there is an active pipeline of internal candidates, hiring from within is a no-brainer. Internal candidates already have knowledge of the company, its culture, and people. Hiring from within is cheaper, faster, and sends a strong message internally regarding career planning. However, as cited in Chapter 2, there are also inherent challenges to promoting from within, including turf struggles, jealousy, and the potential potholes in managing former peers or superiors.

An example of an internal promotion that failed is the case of Disney's chief operating officer (COO) Thomas Staggs. Staggs was identified as the successor to Robert Iger and was put into the COO position three years before Iger was expected to retire. Unfortunately, the transition was handled poorly. The two men's positions overlapped and kept bumping into each other. Ultimately, Staggs left in frustration because it was clear that Iger was not ready to hand over the reins.[2]

There are also times when hiring from outside is appealing and necessary. The absence of internal candidates is usually the driving feature when considering an outside hire. However, there are times when a fresh perspective is needed to "shake up" an organization. A radical example of this occurred when Jeff Immelt at GE hired 5,000 engineers and 5,000 salespeople in 2001, in order to help drive a culture of innovation.[3] External hires can offer a fresh perspective and new ways of working. They are also not wedded to existing, often legacy, processes. However, external hires have a steep learning curve when it comes to understanding the company, people, and key issues with which they will have to deal. Research has found that external hires are 61 percent more likely to be fired or laid off and 21 percent more likely than internal hires to voluntarily resign.[4]

Selection Blunders: Too Fast, Too Slow, or Misaligned

Every opening in a company provides leaders an opportunity to rethink the position in terms of scope and value in the context of organizational goals. Thinking broadly about filling a position allows leaders to change the role and even the impact the position will have on its team or company. However, leaders often underestimate the importance of each and every position in their organization, and thereby lose the opportunity to heighten the impact of incoming employees. We have found that leaders often fall into one of three categories when making hiring decisions.

The Expedient Manager

The expedient manager just wants to get open positions filled as quickly as possible, and with as little disruption to his or her own routines as he or she can get away with. These managers essentially want someone else, usually from human resources or recruiting, to do the work of filling the position for them. They want their involvement to be cursory and are happy to put their stamp of approval on the first passable candidate. They may be desperate, and often have the experience of "glad for now, sorry forever," when they realize they have hired the wrong person.

The Single-Track Manager

These managers are involved in the hiring process and help create specifications for the job, but focus solely on technical capabilities to match candidates to positions. They neglect to look at personal characteristics that are important for an individual to be successful in relation to his or her larger team. Single-track managers would be content entering their stack of resumes into a computer algorithm and selecting the candidate whose technical proficiencies align with the job description. These managers fail to look at, and match, the interpersonal aspects of the person to the job.

Figure 6.1 The expedient manager

Source: andrewgenn/Depositphotos.com. http://depositphotos.com/62762553/stock-illustration-complicated-decisions.html (accessed February 12, 2017).

The Obsessive Manager

These managers are looking for perfection in their hires. They are compulsive about every detail of the position description, both technical and interpersonal. They are characterized by taking excessively long times to get information to and from the sourcing folks. They overfocus on every possible detail down to the font on a candidate's resume, and often interview many candidates, finding some fault with each one. Obsessive managers are the opposite of the expedient manager and tend to "major on minors." They are so fearful of making the wrong decision in their quest to find the perfect candidate that they lose valuable time overlooking candidates who would have been very good for the job. The irony is, of course, that perfect candidates simply do not exist.

It is important for leaders to be involved in all aspects of their people's development, beginning in the hiring phase. Making a bad hiring decision is expensive. According to a 2003 U.S. Department of Labor statistic, a bad hiring decision can equal 30 percent of the individual's first-year potential earnings.[5] In addition, there is disruption to the organization and additional loss of focus and/or productivity with new hires that do not succeed!

The Four Most Common Hiring Mistakes

Virtually every company with which we consult identifies talent development and succession planning as key initiatives. These companies are typically guilty of making the same mistake: putting a function such as human resources in charge of succession planning. On the surface, our calling this a misalignment may seem to be heresy, certainly to human resource professionals! However, we believe that managers at all levels in a company should be held responsible for the talent in their organizations and not "in-source" the task to human resources. When a function is in charge of the talent in the organization, several potential problems emerge, including:

- Hiring decisions are made at a distance from where the work is taking place.
- Hiring managers abdicate responsibility for both the quality of the hire and the subsequent development of their people.
- The *chain-of-accountability* for the success of the new hire becomes blurred.
- Most importantly, in hiring for new positions, there is a tendency to fill positions according to skills and not "fit."

The failure rate for hiring from outside a company, known as organ rejection, is high. According to Mark Murphy, CEO of Leadership IQ, their research of over 20,000 new hires found that 46 percent of new hires fail within the first 18 months. Even more disturbing is the fact that only 11 percent of these failures were due to a lack of skill. The other 89 percent of these failures were due to *attitudinal reasons*, including lack of coachability and low levels of emotional intelligence, motivation, and temperament.[6]

In April 2013, JCPenney's board of directors terminated their CEO, Ron Johnson, after only 17 months on the job. Johnson had been seen as a genius of retail, based on his extraordinary success with Apple's retail stores and their Genius Bar. He had prior experience as the vice president of merchandising at Target and was the architect of their very successful "affordable chic" high-design, low-cost merchandising and marketing strategy.[7] Johnson's failure was seen as one of the perils of hiring executives from the outside who appear to have the technical skills required but are not vetted for the culture fit necessary for success.

Johnson's failures included:[8]

- Misreading what shoppers wanted
- Not testing ideas in advance
- Alienating core customers
- Misunderstanding the JCPenney brand
- Not seeming to like or respect the JCPenney culture

As Johnson's tenure with JCPenney illustrates, the success of a leader in one company or set of circumstances is not necessarily generalizable to another company, position, or challenge. This leads us to the question at the heart of the hiring process. If even past successes are not a sure indicator of future successes, what is the best way to go about creating a team? What is the best way to safeguard the sustained success of your company and what pitfalls should you expect? Our hiring framework rests on a simple foundation. When hiring, more attention needs to be given to a candidate's characteristics that exist outside of his or her requisite skills for the position!

Hiring Mistake #1: The Blueprint Is Not the Building

Most companies begin by trying to fill vacant positions from within. Human resource leaders, often in collaboration with line leaders, construct elaborate schemes to fill future positions. Complex organizational charts filled with zigzagging arrows and rectangles plot out potential "successors" two or three levels down. Incredible amounts of money are invested in human resource information system (HRIS) software programs. Lengthy meetings are held discussing the organization's talent with management, creating high-potential lists, and on, and on. Months of work and hours of time can be sunk into plotting the uncertain hiring future. While many of these initiatives may have some merit, they all lack two critical elements: ownership and follow-up. In company after company, human resources leads the effort, but no one owns the outcomes! As a result, leaders become perplexed and frustrated when, time and again, they are forced to go outside of their organization to fill vacant positions.

A large, complicated, and multilevel organization chart on someone's wall becomes forgotten soon after talent discussion meetings. The HRIS that was supposed to be able to do virtually everything is implemented over budget, behind schedule, and fails to live up to the sales hype. Many of the identified high-potential employees leave the company, exasperated that they have been identified as future leaders but virtually nothing has changed in their jobs, positions, or attention from management. This only perpetuates the problem of not having the right internal people, at the right time, to fill vacant positions.

Hiring Mistake #2: Why the Architect Is Not the General Contractor

A second, and equally confounding problem, arises when hiring from the outside is outsourced to an executive search firm. Unless a search firm has a long-term relationship with an employer and knows the company's people, culture, and strategy, it is not likely to produce candidates who are a good "fit" as described earlier. To be fair, search firms are often working from a job description or list of capabilities and trying to match candidates to these lists. They source from their extensive databases or contacts and, typically, produce two to three candidates for the position. The unspoken dilemma is that, while these may be the best candidates from the universe of the search firm, they are not necessarily the best candidates from the universe of potential candidates.

Much like realtors, search firms have the desire to close the deal, produce an acceptable candidate, and move on to their next search. They have little stake in the success of the candidate once the position is filled. After all, their payday comes when the position is filled, not when the candidate is successful five years down the line. Increasingly, ethical search firms are taking more responsibility for the success of their candidates by assisting with the onboarding process and offering to conduct a subsequent search, free of charge, if the candidate fails within a specified time period. Ultimately, however, the selection of the right candidate needs to rest on the shoulders of the hiring manager, not on a search firm or human resources department.

Hiring Mistake #3: The Facade Is Not the Structure

It is often the case that a hiring manager and a candidate seem to "click." They seem to be able to talk easily, have many things in common, and the hiring manager feels an emotional connection with the candidate. We have a positive bias for people similar to us. Rather than providing comfort, this "connection" should raise red flags! The candidate has a vested interest in having the hiring manager like them. The degree to which they want the position is closely related to the degree of appeal or charisma the candidate evidences. This is particularly true for extroverts who specialize in being gregarious and likeable. This positive bias for people like us can also, unconsciously, create other biases such as gender and racial bias. It is a tendency to be aware of and to manage in the hiring process.

While being liked is certainly not a negative in itself, it is not usually a good sign when an interview moves quickly from the requirements of the job to more personal, and entertaining, topics. The focus of the interview can become lost while savoring the social connection of the conversation. The question of the candidate's fit for the job in terms of temperament, coachability, and emotional intelligence can become lost. The manager can easily mistake this likability for capability, and that is a fallacious conclusion! By preparing for each interview with a list of characteristics for "fit" and focusing on questions that will elicit that information, managers can avoid this entertainment trap.

A related difficulty is the manager's own need to be liked. Leaders can mistake feeling good about an interview for candidate qualifications. When candidates praise the hiring manager, whom they have just met, it can be a way of trying to curry favor rather than genuine admiration of the manager. Those hiring managers who are vulnerable to this kind of adulation will often make choices based on the wrong set of criteria. It is understandable that, when we hear something we enjoy hearing from candidates, we tend to assign a positive bias to them. However, both liking a candidate and being liked by a candidate should be only of very small weight in the final hiring decision.

Hiring Mistake #4: Why You Should Not Choose Your Own Successor

When working with a group of individuals over time, it is common to develop relationships and alliances that have both breadth and depth to them. Over time, subtle, often unconscious, biases develop on the part of leaders regarding members on their team. Characteristics like working hard, producing results that please the leader, or being likable, create biases on the part of the leader. However, these are not the same traits that make an employee a good leader.

In addition, the more similar employees are to their leader, the more the leader may favor them. This bias can also happen in reverse. Those unlike us or who have different ways of working, thinking, or getting results can create an unconscious negative prejudice. These biases, and preexisting relationships with an outgoing leader, put the leader in a tenuous position for selecting his or her successor. The person who gets along best with a certain leader is not necessarily the best person to be in power at an organization. As a result, when selecting a successor, the incumbent is not a good choice for having the last word when selecting the next person to occupy the position. Typically, the manager's manager should be the primary person, in consultation with other key leaders, to make the succession decision.

Ultimately, if a leader has been focused on developing his or her team over the long haul, there will always be a pool of talent from which to choose successors. This focus on development of employees is also good for the business. What business ever suffers from having too much talent?

Case Study

Mistaking Similarities for Fit

A tight knit, family-owned carpet manufacturer was experiencing the retirement of its president, a 30-year employee who had risen through the ranks. The founder, a bright but reclusive woman who had operated at arm's length for some time, determined that she would become involved in the process of selecting the next president. When it was clear that there were no suitable internal candidates, she hired an external search firm to conduct the search. The search firm met with the founder and a couple of her top staff members to determine the qualifications for the position. It was determined that a good candidate would be someone currently in a small, family-owned business with a financial background (like the previous president) that was ready to move up. After a brief exploration, the search firm presented the founder with a couple of ostensibly suitable choices. The founder quickly identified, and zeroed-in on, a candidate working for a family-owned wood and tile flooring company. The founder requested that we evaluate the candidate to provide additional data. Our evaluation determined that the candidate was not a good fit for the position, given her propensity to gloss over details and her tendency to be too boisterous for the introverted founder. We predicted their differing interpersonal styles would lead to workplace clashes. Nonetheless, the founder hired her, enamored with the fact that she was already doing a similar job at a smaller company. The new hire was on the job for six months when the founder called to say that she regretted ignoring both our concerns and the counsel of her staff. She conceded that the

(Continued)

new president was simply not working out. The founder, embarrassed that she had not heeded any of the dissenting counsel, determined to go back to the drawing board. She vowed that the next set of candidates would be considered not only for their business acumen and background, but also for their fit with the culture, and most importantly, for their fit with her personally. With our help, the next hiring went far more smoothly and, while not perfect, the match was much better for the company and for the founder.

Hiring Well: From Resume Through First Day

Leaders who have created high-performing teams have spent an extraordinary amount of time in the selection, and *deselection*, process. They are clear about the kind of culture that exists in their organizations and have spent time understanding the differences between those who have been successful and those who are not. They are committed to having people on their teams who will heighten the success of the organization and not simply meet the basic requirement of success. They typically have a comprehensive plan and process for selecting candidates. Pulling from our experiences with hundreds of hiring managers, we have identified the four most important steps of the hiring process.

Step #1: Evaluate for Fit

Extraordinary leaders take time to pinpoint the key components that will lead to success in a job. Most job descriptions have boilerplate descriptions of characteristics so numerous that only a saint could fulfill them. Strong leaders take time to highlight only those characteristics critical to success in a position. Interestingly, the technical characteristics of a job, in most cases, are less important than the nontechnical aspects. While there are jobs that absolutely require a very clear set of technical capabilities, there is a wider berth for most positions. As the research we have cited suggests, success in a position is more related to things like motivation, attitude, ability to work well with others, energy, drive, and communication skills. The wise manager considers these skills first and technical skills second. As Heinz von Foerster suggested, it is much easier to teach technical skills than the "soft skills."

Step #2: Interviewing for Fit

When hiring for "fit," rather than for technical acumen, the hiring manager interviews in a much different manner. The interview focuses on how well the candidate relates and thinks, and not as much on the candidate's education, previous experience, or credentials. Behavioral interviewing using the STAR method (Situation, Task, Action, Result) can be very enlightening in uncovering *how* a candidate behaves in different situations. The candidate is asked to provide an example of a complex business situation from his or her past, the task or specifics of what was required, the actions taken by the candidate, and the result, with detail on metrics and impact. The interviewer listens for *how* the work was carried out; the result is extraneous. Do candidates cite how they worked with others, how they overcame unusual circumstances, and how they communicated with their teams? The interviewer listens for whether they take or share credit and for the strength of their resolve in the face of challenges. This kind of interview provides the manager with a wealth of knowledge beyond merely understanding if the candidate's education and technical background match the position. It gives the manager greater insight into whether or not the candidate will be likely to succeed in the position.

Step #3: Third-Party Assessment

Even with the best interviewing and internal evaluation of a candidate's fit for a position, subtle but important personality traits can still be missed or overlooked. Having an external expert skilled in assessing candidates can provide hiring managers good insight into candidates that they would not otherwise have. Research has demonstrated that around three quarters of companies larger than 100 employees use evaluations such as aptitude and personality tests for external hiring.[9] Behavioral components such as motivation, critical thinking, interpersonal competence, and creativity are areas for which these assessments provide insights. Organizational psychologists are particularly skilled at evaluating candidates and providing additional data points in the hiring process. When considering using external third-party experts for assessing candidates, it is important to ensure that assessments meet validity, reliability, and Equal Employment Opportunity (EEO) guidelines. Using external candidate assessments can further ensure the success of the hired candidate. Such external evaluators differ positively from search firms in that they are enhancing your knowledge of your selected talent pool rather than restricting whom you are looking at.

Step #4: Onboarding

For years, new employees have been subjected to an orientation consisting of a day of dull classes and lectures on company policy, receiving and using a computer, description of benefits, and so on. This is a necessary evil to familiarize the new employee with the fundamentals of just getting through the first day of work. Until recently, much less attention has been given to actually "onboarding" new employees. Onboarding new employees requires the manager, or a third party, to help the new employee understand the business goals, challenges, and objectives they are going to face. The onboarding process should also help the new employees understand the team they will manage and help them create a 100-day plan on which to focus in their new position. The more detail that can be provided, the more likely the new manager will be successful.

Leaders who are successful at building high-performing organizations know that it is all about the talent on their teams. They know that there is nothing more important than spending time on selecting the right talent for the right job, including their fit with the goals and culture of the organization. Carefully introducing a new employee to the specific challenges and opportunities of their new job and helping them create a plan will shorten their learning curve and accelerate their effectiveness. Building a pipeline of talent to sustain, and grow, the business is the most important area of any leader's focus.

The Changing Environment in Selection

Over the course of the past several years, the hiring landscape has changed dramatically. This change is, in part, due to a robust economy creating greater job demand than worker supply. Other factors include an aging, and shrinking, workforce; the advent of the Affordable Care Act (impacting companies with over 50 employees); and the growth of both consulting firms and temporary staffing services. The changing landscape is also due to the emergence of millennials and the expectations they have for work. We believe that these factors represent a paradigm shift requiring hiring managers to think fundamentally differently about whom they put into vacant positions and how they go about it.

How to Talk to People Who Have Never Used a Landline Phone or Seen a Record Player

Much has been written of millennials in the workplace. Countless think pieces and blog entries have tried to solve the riddle of this alien generation that grocery shops with iphone apps and thinks CDs are ancient technology. They have changed workplace expectations in ways that have mystified their baby boomer managers. The truth behind Millennial ideology, however, is rather simple and reflects shifts in twenty-first-century technology and culture rather than expressing something entirely new. Millennials seek to bring to the workplace the flexible and freer lifestyle that they were raised with in the post–cold war era. It is estimated that up to 34 percent of today's workforce is made up of this age group and, by 2020, nearly half (46 percent) of all U.S. workers will be millennials.[10] They tend to get married later in life, are more educated, more in debt, more racially diverse, and tend to be more tolerant of differences than previous generations. Here is what you need to know about their workplace expectations.

- They require greater work–life balance. They work to live and expect more time away from work.
- They are committed, but not loyal in the traditional sense; they will move to another job if it offers perks more in line with their lifestyles.
- They expect to be rewarded for their efforts, including quicker promotions, raises, and so on.
- They feel more comfortable expressing their individuality than previous generations.

- They expect to communicate through technology more than previous generations.
- They have different views on how to schedule their work.

Along with these expectations, millennials bring skills that older generations do not. Their familiarity with social media assists them in communicating rapidly, and with a larger group than previous generations. They tend to communicate more informally, but also more succinctly. They are open, creative, and willing to challenge the status quo. They are more willing to take risks and experiment. Like previous generations, they also want to make a difference both at work and away from work. When hiring and developing millennials, hiring managers will want to keep several things in mind.

Hire for the present. Understand that when you are hiring millennials, they are likely to be more interested in the work or the project than opportunities for advancement or a multiyear career opportunity.

Manage first impression biases. The expectations of older-generation hiring managers often lag behind societal norms. It is important to see beyond tattoos and body piercings to the substantive skills and capabilities candidates possess.

Be flexible in scheduling. This will test the manager's ability to truly empower employees. Let them know your expectations but allow them to accomplish them in the way they work best. They may leave work early and arrive late. Keep in mind that the objective is to have them complete assignments on time with acceptable quality and quantity, and that this flex-

"We're doing everything you guys did—marriage, career, children-only in reverse."

Figure 6.2 The millennials

Source: andrewgenn/Depositphotos.com. http://depositphotos.com/70281747/stock-illustration-family-generations.html (accessed February 12, 2016).

ibility will likely *increase* this possibility. This includes a willingness for managers to allow telecommuting.

Provide meaningful work. Give them assignments that are meaningful and for which they can receive recognition. They will respond better, and remain more engaged, working on higher-profile projects. Allow them to take risks and innovate.

Communicate with them. Even though their primary communication may be electronic, they will benefit from, and appreciate, face time with their manager.

Collaborate. They will work well with others as long as office politics and drama are kept to a minimum. They will tend to work well with others on team projects.

Most of these approaches are applicable to employees of any generation and will lead to increased productivity and employee satisfaction. The difference with millennials is that they have learned to demand what other generations may have simply enjoyed.

Not All Vacancies Require Hiring: Managing Transient Help

When a vacancy exists, it is an opportunity for leaders to consider whether or not the position needs to be filled by a permanent hire or temporary help. This is a time to consider if it would be beneficial to shift from a fixed to a variable expense, based on the work to be done. Temporary staffing agencies exist for virtually all levels and positions in an organization from CEO to the manufacturing line. This should be given consideration any time an opening occurs. Questions to consider when making the decision include:

- Does the position require a full-time employee?
- Does the position require institutional knowledge or specialized technical skills?
- Does the leader want to experiment with changing the focus of the position without having to invest significantly?

- Would the manager like to "test drive" an employee for the position before hiring?
- Is the position a new one that needs to be better defined before hiring a permanent employee?

The chart in Figure 6.3 will provide guidance on when less-than-full-time help would be desirable. The goal is to manage both cost and control of a position.

All temporary assignments need to have a clear and written contract detailing work to be done, time frames, fees, and deliverables. It is not unusual for managers to experience "scope creep" from both consultants and contractors, involving work that is conducted outside of the original scope of work that requires an additional fee.

A second, but common problem, is "scope seep" in which the manager identifies additional work for the temporary worker to accomplish "as long as you are here." Scope seep can dilute the original work in the contract and lead to unforeseen expenses. In both cases, a new scope of work is required and managers must hold contractors and/or consultants accountable for agreed-upon deliverables.

The forward-thinking, strategic leader is always considering creative solutions for what their organization needs and how to achieve its goals. When opportunities arise to fill vacancies, they consider all options and are careful not to become misled by company history or prior expectations. Bringing in temporary assistance can be one of those options.

Assignment	Type of hire			
	Full-time	Temporary	Contractor	Consultant
Replacement	X			
Short/Routine	X	X		
Short/Technical		X	X	
Long/Routine	X		X	X
Long/Technical	X	X	X	
New position	X	X		

Figure 6.3 Hiring grid

Coach's Corner

One of the most important decisions in business is hiring the right person for the right position. If all candidates were equally suited for all businesses and positions, the work of organizations would almost take care of itself. It is the people whom businesses employ that will ultimately determine whether the business is successful over the long term.

Four Tips for Hiring the Right Person

1. **Empower your hiring manager**
   - Outsourcing hiring decisions primarily to human resources committees or external search firms ultimately dilutes accountability. It should be the hiring manager who has the final say and is incentivized directly to find the right employee.
2. **Hire for fit**
   - Technical capabilities are a bare minimum for determining suitability. It is the intangibles such as interpersonal fit and critical problem-solving abilities that make the difference. Use personality evaluations and behavioral interviewing techniques to help determine fit.
3. **Likeability versus suitability**
   - The likeability of an interviewing candidate should be taken with a grain of salt. It often says more about the hiring manager than the candidate's suitability for the open position. Stick with concrete rather than social questions to avoid this trap.
4. **Hiring as an opportunity**
   - Use open positions as an opportunity to fundamentally rethink the scope and goals of their job description. Think of ways in which realigning an open position could better serve your organization's goals and mission.

Chapter 6 Survey

Difficult conversations	Much too little	Barely too little	Just right	Barely too much	Much too much
Please insert an "X" in the appropriate box to indicate your answer	-4	-3	-2	-1	0	+1	+2	+3	+4
To what extent do you consider interpersonal qualities when hiring a new employee?									
To what extent does your desire to fill vacant positions effect who you're willing to hire?									
How much do you rely on outside functions or firms to help in your hiring process?									

Areas for Development

What are the top three ways you can adjust your hiring process to better fill roles and serve your organization's goals.

1. _____

2. _____

3. _____

Notes

1. von Foerster (2016).
2. Bradt (2016).
3. Schonfeld (2004).
4. Bidwell (2011).
5. Holmes (2013).
6. Murphy (2015).
7. Tichy (2014).
8. Tuttle (2013).
9. Chamorro-Premuzic (2015).
10. Lynch (2008).

References

Bidwell, M. 2011. "Paying More to Get Less: The Effects of External Hiring versus Internal Mobility." *Administrative Science Quarterly* 56, no. 3, pp. 369–407.

Bradt, G. 2016. "Learning for Disney's Staggering Succession Failure." *Forbes*, April 5. *http://forbes.com/sites/georgebradt/2016/04/05/learning-from-disneys-staggering-ceo-succession-failure.html* (accessed February 12, 2016).

Chamorro-Premuzic, T. 2015. "Ace the Assessment." *Harvard Business Review*, July-August, pp.118–21.

Holmes, R. 2013. "The Unexpectedly High Cost of a Bad Hire." *LinkedIn*, July 16. *https://linkedin.com/.../20130716151946-2967511-the-high-costs-of-a-bad-hire.html* (accessed February 12, 2016).

Lynch, A. 2008. "ROI on Generation Y Employees." *Bottom Line Conversations, LLC.* Retrieved February 12, 2016 from *http://knoxvillechamber.com/pdf/workforce/ROIonGenYWhitePaper.pdf*

Murphy, M. 2015. "Why New Hires Fail (Emotional Intelligence Vs. Skills)." *The Blog by Mark Murphy and Leadership IQ*, June 22. *http://leadershipiq. com/blogs/leadershipiq/35354241-why-new-hires-fail-emotional-intelligence-vs-skills?.html* (accessed February 12, 2016).

Schonfeld, E. 2004. "GE Sees the Light By learning to manage innovation, Jeffrey Immelt is remaking America's flagship industrial corporation into a technology and marketing powerhouse." *CNN Money*, July 1. http://money. cnn.com/magazines/business2/business2_archive/2004/07/01/374824.html (accessed February 12, 2016).

Tichy, N. 2014. "J.C. Penney and the Terrible Costs of Hiring an Outsider CEO." *Fortune*, Nov 13. *http://fortune.com/2014/11/13/jc-penney-ron-johnson-ceo-succession.html* (accessed February 12, 2016).

Tuttle, B. 2013. "The 5 Big Mistakes That Led to Ron Johnson's Ouster at JC Penney." *Time*, April 9. *http://business.time.com/2013/04/09/the-5-big-mistakes-that-led-to-ron-johnsons-ouster-at-jc-penney.html* (accessed February 12, 2016).

von Foerster, H. 2016. *AZ Quotes. www.azquotes.com* (accessed February 12, 2016).

CHAPTER 7

The Disciplines of Communication: Maximizing Impact and Productivity

In our work with companies across industries, the most often cited area for improvement in companies is communication. Employees consistently complain that the information they receive that is required for them to do their jobs arrives too late, too little, and often too obscure. They often lament that they find out about issues that directly impact them from outside sources, external social media sites, and sometimes even on the nightly news! But communication problems are not just a nuisance, they may prove costly the business. Studies have attributed poor communication to such things as sickness and absentee rates, reduced customer satisfaction, and increased information technology (IT) costs.[1] In other words, poor communication goes beyond just being a frustration to resulting in real cost to the business.

In consulting with people at all levels of business, the most common criticism we hear is that they wish their organizations, managers, and leaders were better at communicating. This criticism takes many forms, but it is ultimately centered on the belief that employees are not given enough information to do their jobs in a timely manner. Complaints range from not being included on e-mail lists to hearing, for the first time, about something they directly manage in a large meeting and being caught off guard and embarrassed—such as one American chief executive officer (CEO) who did not find out about the large Canadian call center his sales manager had opened until a shareholder meeting. In addition to the absence of such important communication, they also cite concerns that, when they do get information, it can be irrelevant, overdetailed, unclear or delivered in the wrong form. There are times when it makes a big difference whether information is communicated in person, by a telephone call, or written message.

"Have you met Mr. Hand, the head of communications?"

Figure 7.1 The perils of miscommunication

Source: andrewgenn/Depositphotos.com. http://depositphotos. com/62875141/stock-illustration-vector-puppet-as-head-of. html (accessed on January 10, 2017).

An example of miscommunication occurred at the annual meeting of the procurement department of a major manufacturing organization. The vice president in charge of the function rolled out a new organization chart for the upcoming year, detailing changes in status and function for all employees in the room. While reorganizations are common in business, in this case, the vice president *had not discussed changes with anyone who would be impacted by the reorganization!* The clumsy vice president was forced to watch in horror as those who had lost responsibilities, status, and power visibly sank into their seats. It was nearly as embarrassing and uncomfortable for those who were being elevated into new and greater roles. It was a case study of how *not* to roll out a new organization and resulted in the vice president needing to spend a great deal of time and effort doing damage control. Obviously, do not do it this way!

Communication is so fundamental to working with others that it is perplexing why it would need more discussion. Lack of proper communication is not constrained to the social and ecological situations stated earlier alone; one recent Watson Wyatt study concluded that companies that communicate effectively have a 47 percent higher return to shareholder value over a five-year period.[2] I am sure that, given this information, many employees who have not been informed adequately would say that the study states the obvious!

Leadership Communication: Moving from Haphazard to Intentional

The most fundamental of all leadership skills is the ability to communicate effectively. However, most leaders do not employ the *discipline* of communication. As they move up in organizations, leaders tend to take for granted that the informal and haphazard way they have communicated in previous positions will be adequate in their new position. In fact, it is rarely the case that leaders even consider that communication is an important discipline that requires serious attention and must be used carefully, in order for them and their organizations to be most effective. This inattention to communicating precisely causes organizations to lose focus, creates unnecessary duplication of efforts, and results in hours of time lost with employees unaware of exactly what their superiors want.

The central purpose of business communication is to get *the right information to the right people at the right time*. While this would not seem to be too difficult, there are three types of violators to these communication requirements.

The Sparse Communicator

This type of communication violator is typified by consistently providing less information than is necessary. They may see themselves as being too busy or assume that everyone knows what they should be doing. They are not in the habit of delivering information, not discerning about what to communicate, or do not understand what information is needed by those in their organization to accomplish initiatives. The single unifying element is that these violators seriously underestimate the negative impact of their teams not having sufficient information to do their jobs. The discipline these individuals lack is an awareness of just how harmful their lack of communication is to their team's performance. They then often misattribute their team's underperformance to deficits in the individuals on the team, rather than to their own lack of providing sufficient information in a timely manner.

The Excessive Communicator

This individual often *mistakes activity for productivity*. They can be very social, highly verbal, and fluent with technology. Their communications are frequent, full of information, and delivered to everyone, both in person and through e-mails. In their view, everything is both urgent and important to everyone in the organization. They are as likely to communicate team goals as send an office-wide memo on what brand of coffee filters ought to be supplied in the break room. As a result, the recipients of their barrage of information become buried in material and become paralyzed by information overload. These excessive communicators have constantly changing priorities. They often act with a CYA mentality so that their superiors will not be able to blame them if something goes wrong. After all, they have communicated everything imaginable to their organizations. These individuals do not take the time to sort through and triage information in order to make concise and targeted communications to the right people. They lack the discipline of prioritizing and discernment.

The Poor Communicator

Somewhere in between the sparse and the excessive communicators are those individuals who may take their time to carefully select the information they should send and target their recipients, but simply happen to be poor communicators. These individuals may lack clarity, be too abstract, or provide only partial information. Their employees may view them as well intentioned, but completely ineffective at getting necessary information across. The result of ongoing poor communication is that the team continues to be perplexed as to the direction in which they should be moving.

Regardless of whether a leader provides too little, too much, or poorly communicated information, the outcome will be the same. Their teams will have difficulty prioritizing their work and understanding how to focus their efforts to accomplish the goals of the organization.

The Disciplines of Communication: Simple Rules

Leaders must develop better communication skills to provide the right material to the right people at the right time, and thereby give their teams a chance to perform at a high level. Our experience helping leaders communicate more effectively focuses on a few simple basics that set the stage for optimizing the impact of their messages, targeting recipients carefully and reducing the number of messages they send.

Case Study

Too Much Information Already!

The chief operating officer (COO) of an international manufacturer of motorcycle parts was promoted to the role of president upon the retirement of his long-term and beloved predecessor. This promotion was a measured move that had been part of the company's succession-planning process, and the transition was expected to occur seamlessly. However, as the COO assumed the role of president, he continued to do more of what had made him successful in his previous position, and that was paying high levels of attention to the details of the business.

In filling his previous role, the new president had to go outside of the organization because no internal candidates were ready to move up. Once the new COO was hired, the president set aside time to help him understand his new role—or so the president thought. At the beginning of their first meeting, the president gave the COO a 40-page PowerPoint, outlining all of the president's priorities. Each page had four items that required attention. In other words, the new COO became responsible for 160 *priorities*. Four hours later, the new COO left the president's office totally overwhelmed and discouraged, wondering just what he had gotten himself into!

The COO called us for counsel on just how to deal with the situation. He reviewed the president's large presentation and vented his frustration. Over the next few months, we worked with the new COO to create a process for classifying the 160 issues into areas of importance and timeliness. Subsequently, he had a series of meetings with the president and, together, they worked out a way to meaningfully prioritize the issues that mattered most, and forget about some that did not. The COO was able to work on those issues of greatest importance in a manner that kept him from being overwhelmed or frustrated, resulting in a better sense of accomplishment. Admittedly, the road to improvement was rocky as the president learned how to communicate with headlines and the COO learned to provide more detail than he would have normally.

(Continued)

The organization learned that simply having a succession plan in place is not enough. The best laid plans when poorly communicated become ineffective. Moving forward, the organization vowed to couple its onboarding of top executives with properly communicated directives. Today, they supply parts to some of the biggest names in the motorcycle business.

Discipline 1: Differentiating

The first discipline requires that the leader characterize the data with which they are confronted. They must take the time to review and organize the information they will deliver. There are generally four categories of communications:

- Information only: Material in this category is often delivered to multiple people, often in blast e-mails and with broad application. Frequently no action is required as in announcing the time and place of events such as a fire drill. These messages should always be short and to the point. Little attention is required from the leader for examination.
- Problem-solving: These communications are typically sent to a narrower range of people who are involved in specific initiatives or tasks. These communications, if sent electronically, should not include any interpersonal issues that should only be discussed face-to-face (see Chapter 5).
- Follow-up: This category relates to documenting agreements from prior conversations or meetings, ownership of issues, expectations, and timelines. Follow-up communications are always sent to only a select group of those who have been previously informed.
- Action required: In these communications, there is some specific action required of the recipient. Obviously, these communications are only sent to those involved with the request/demand.

All of the aforementioned can be intended only for those inside a company or can include those outside a company such as customers, vendors, press, and so on. Obviously, special care needs to be given to wording of documents in external communications, to prevent any potential misunderstanding, backlash, or harm.

In sorting through the material with which a leader is presented, he or she will want to ensure that the right communications go *only* to the right people. In our technologically charged world where it is estimated that the average worker spends up to 6.3 hours per day just checking e-mails, fewer, concise, and targeted communications are required.[3] Most importantly, determining whether or not a message is worthy of being sent, or resent, is the best use of differentiating. The leader needs to understand that in sending messages or communications to multiple recipients, the leader is multiplying the time spent by those audiences. This is really a case of time having a dollar value to it. Furthermore, each additional communication sent to the same person decreases the likelihood of that person reading and responding to all communications he or she received. The best leader is always the discerning leader, sending targeted communications to only those who need it.

Discipline 2: Language

Every leader needs to ensure that each message he or she crafts says exactly what it is intended to say. In general, crafting messages in the most succinct manner possible, while making sure the topic is covered, saves time for recipients and is more likely to hold their attention. People tune out when messages are overly detailed or excessively elaborated. One guideline is to provide mainly the headlines and let your audience determine whether or not they want more of the story. This is particularly true with in-person communication. Every company or industry has its own set of acronyms and complex language that has meaning to some, but not all, individuals in an organization. Effective leaders ensure that their messages are free from as much jargon or technical terms as possible, in order to be understood by a broad reader base.

An example of a poorly constructed memo was one sent in February 2013 to all Yahoo employees by the head of human resources (HR), informing employees that telecommuting was no longer acceptable at Yahoo. Employees were required to either find a local office to work out of or quit, without exception! This memo failed to explain the rationale behind it, leaving Yahoo employees upset and frustrated. Had more attention been provided to the language and construction of the memo, the subsequent backlash could have been reduced or managed more effectively.[4]

Discipline 3: Audience

It is essential to take the time to best determine those who will benefit most from an intended message. Delivering messages to specific audiences is the most efficient, but one of the least used disciplines. Sparse communicators tend to send communications to too few individuals, often leaving out others who critically need to receive the message. Excessive communicators find it easier to reply "send all," but the downstream waste of time and energy does not justify including the entire group. In addition, always assume that any information you send electronically may be shared with, or intercepted by, others besides the intended recipients. Take care that your electronic communication will not be likely misinterpreted if it is read by parties other than those intended.

An example of when greater audience discernment should have been used was in August 2013 when AOL Chief Executive Officer (CEO) Tim Armstrong announced that AOL would be reducing the number of Patch websites. Soon afterward, Armstrong spoke to 1,000 employees on a conference call that was intended to boost their morale and discuss the future. What happened instead was far from morale boosting.

Armstrong ended up firing Patch's creative director, Abel Lenz, in front of everyone. Four days after he fired Lenz, Armstrong sent AOL employees an apology for his behavior. However, he made excuses for his behavior rather than owning up to it and sharing what he learned.[5]

Discipline 4: Delivery

Determining the method used to deliver your communication depends, in part, on the nature and complexity of the message. The simpler the message, the easier it is to send through e-mail. More complex material, requiring greater discussion, should be sent prior to any meeting for study and review. The more problem-solving required, the more the necessity

Message	Modality				
	Person-to-Person	Phone	Video conference	E-mail/Written	Tweet/Text
Informational/Simple	X	X	X	X	X
Informational/Complex	X	X	X		
Personal	X	X	X		
Confidential	X	X	X		
Problem-solving	X	X	X		

Figure 7.2 Message by modality grid

for face-to-face conversations (including video conferencing). Most of all, never use technology to send emotionally charged messages. Any emotionally charged or conflictual messages require face-to-face and, preferably, in-person communication.

When considering what delivery system to use, Figure 7.2 provides a decision grid to assist in choosing which modality to use. Note that some types of messages are appropriate for multiple modalities, while others are better delivered only in a particular modality.

In those messages with multiple modalities, some may require more than one modality (e.g., company news, company or team meetings), while some will require only the best modality (performance discussions, confidential information). Exercising discipline in what modality to use for specific messages will increase the likelihood that the right messages will be sent to the right people in the right time frames. In addition to choosing which modality to use, it is important to exercise caution when sending blast e-mails; using "reply all" when responding to e-mails; and including people when sending or forwarding e-mails who do not need to be copied. Use caution not to publicly reveal private e-mail addresses. The fewer, targeted, succinct messages sent, the better for all.

Discipline 5: Confirmation

Assuring that the communications you deliver are, in fact, received, by requesting that the recipient acknowledge receipt of the message is always a good practice. This closes the loop and prevents responses such as, "I never got the e-mail," or "it must have gone to spam." If you do not receive confirmation of receipt of your communication in a relatively short time, (24 to 48 hours) a follow-up message or a person-to-person conversation would be in order. If, in fact, the message was not received, it is hard to hold someone responsible for responding and it may be necessary to obtain correct contact information.

The most effective leaders take their time to effectively categorize their communications, carefully craft them, and specifically target their audience. Organizations led by excellent communicators have clarity of priorities, are more successful, and are more likely to drive greater shareholder value.

What You Cannot Communicate

A significant part of being a leader is knowing when to communicate and when to withhold information. At times, there are issues that leaders must keep confidential and not discuss with anyone. In some cases, sharing the information could put the business at risk. At other times, the element of surprise becomes a competitive advantage. The following are examples of information that leaders must keep close.

- Mergers and acquisitions (M&A): Often in M&A transactions, both parties sign nondisclosure agreements, which prevent either side from discussing the internal business of either party. In addition, if the Securities and Exchange Commission (SEC) becomes involved, communication can be further restricted regarding document and data security and potential price offerings of targets.
- Pending lawsuits: Whether legal action is internal or external, there are often limits that stipulate what can be made public and what cannot. Always err on the side of being conservative.
- Product launches: The element of surprise is often seen as a competitive advantage. Although many people are usually involved in a product launch, the event must be kept quiet in order to surprise the competition and quickly gain market share.

- Proprietary technology or business processes: When capitalizing on a marketplace advantage by leapfrogging rivals in technology, there is a short window before competitors catch up by reverse-engineering and copying.
- Personnel issues: These can be among the touchiest of issues, especially when the prospect of disciplinary action or termination exists. The potential for legal action in any personnel case requires a high level of confidentiality.
- Future restructuring or downsizing: Companies change workforces and locations for a variety of reasons such as moving overseas, weak business results, opening or closing branches or offices, and so on. Extremely negative consequences can occur when word of impending changes slips out prematurely.
- Insider stock information: The sharing of, and trading on, material, nonpublic information related to impending share price changes, is clearly abuse and should be punished. There have been numerous lawsuits and, even jail sentences, associated with insider stock information getting into hands of outside investors.

Leaders often overestimate the extent to which others will keep their confidences secret and underestimate the negative impact leaks can have. It is also common for leaders to have certain confidants in their organization with whom they have become close. However, it is imperative that information that is expected to be closely held is actually closely held, regardless of personal ties. Leaks occur when leaders talk in confidence with those to whom they are close. Those very people repeat this pattern with those to whom they are close.

We have come to refer to this cycle as the Corkscrew of Trust. Unlike a circle, a corkscrew never closes, and in this way, confidential information can permeate through an entire organization. Before

Figure 7.3 The corkscrew of trust

Source: mangsaab/Depositphotos.com. http://deposit-photos.com/109733872/stock-illustration-business-people-whisper-some-message.html (accessed January 10, 2017).

long, the confidential information becomes prematurely public and may be skewed or misrepresented, creating even more problems.

Coach's Corner

Effective communication ensures that the right teams and people have the information they need when they need it. The most successful leaders take time to carefully craft who receives their communications, and what they communicate. This in turn drives productivity and ultimately increases the shareholder's bottom line.

The Five Disciplines of Communication

Discipline 1: Differentiating

- Organize the information you wish to communicate to ensure that the right communications go *only* to the right people. The most important aspect of differentiating is deciding whether a communication must be sent at all.

Discipline 2: Language

- Craft messages in the most succinct manner possible while making sure the topic is still covered in order to save time for recipients and hold their attention.

Discipline 3: Audience

- Take time to best determine who will benefit most from an intended message. Neither leave out those who critically need to receive the message, nor "send all" when the downstream waste of time and energy does not justify including an entire group.

Discipline 4: Delivery

- The simpler a message, the easier it is to send through e-mail. More complex and personal material are more likely to

require face-to-face conversations. Never use technology to
send emotionally charged messages.

Discipline 5: Confirmation

- Assure that the communications you deliver are, in fact,
  received, by requesting that the recipient acknowledge receipt
  of the message. This closes up possible gaps in communication before they can form.

Areas for Development

As you think about your company, what are the top three ways you can
communicate more effectively?

1. _____

2. _____

3. _____

Chapter 7 Survey

Effective delegation	Much too little		Barely too little		Just right	Barely too much		Much too much	
Please insert an "X" in the appropriate box to indicate your answer	−4	−3	−2	−1	0	+1	+2	+3	+4
How much information do you include in communications?									
How much time do you spend determining who to send communications to?									
How many communications do you send on a daily basis?									

Notes

1. Annan (2017).
2. Baldoni (2009).
3. Naragon (2015).
4. Grossman (2014).
5. Grossman (2013).

References

Annan, L. 2017. "Costs of Poor Workplace Communication." *Business Performance*, accessed March 19. *http://businessperform.com/workplace-communication/poor-communication-costs.html*

Baldoni, J. 2009. "New Study: How Communication Drives Performance." *Harvard Business Review*, November 19. *https://hbr.org/2009/11/new-study-how-communication-dr?html* (accessed January 10, 2017).

Grossman, D. 2013. *"AOL CEO Fires Employee During Call Intended to Boost Morale." Leader Communicator Blog*, August 14. *http://yourthoughtpartner.com/blog/bid/69729/AOL-CEO-Fires-Employee-During-Call-Intended-to-Boost-Morale.html* (accessed January 10, 2017).

Grossman, D. 2014. "The Top 3 Corporate Communication Mistakes of 2013." *Leader Communicator Blog*, January 21. *http://yourthoughtpartner.com/blog/bid/73501/The-Top-3-Corporate-Communication-Mistakes-of-2013* (accessed January 10, 2017).

Naragon, K. 2015. "Subject: Email, We Just Can't Get Enough." *Adobe News*, August 26. *https://blogs.adobe.com/conversations/2015/08/email.html* (accessed January 10, 2017).

CHAPTER 8

The Person in the Mirror: Overcoming Questions about Your Competence

The chief executive officer (CEO) of a large financial services company made a bold invitation to his employees. Noting that it is lonely at the top, and that no one provided him feedback about his performance, he requested that his staff offer him constructive criticism. Taking the CEO at his word, one of his senior staff requested an appointment a few weeks later. Several people had voiced their concerns to this staff member about the CEO's abrasive behavior and the impact it had on staff morale. The senior staff member decided to summon her courage, and at the appointed time, marched into the CEO's office. After some brief chit-chat and business news, the senior staff asked the CEO if he would like some feedback in light of his previous request. The CEO sat up in his seat, looking earnest but open, and said "sure." The senior staff member voiced her concern about the CEO's abrasive behavior and wondered if there was anything she could do to help alleviate any stress the CEO may be experiencing. The CEO quickly became angry and defensive, saying that the senior staff's information was incorrect, and he summarily dismissed her from his office. Stunned, the staff member left the CEO's office vowing to herself never to repeat this mistake! The senior staff had tapped into the CEO's greatest fear, that his shortcomings had been spotted and he had not been able to hide his flaws from others. In spite of his request for feedback, he was caught off guard and his insecurities came screaming through.

The Ubiquity of Insecurity

Everyone experiences *bouts of insecurity*, especially when faced with situations that have some level of importance. This is particularly true when they feel powerless, unprepared, or incompetent. This kind of insecurity is usually fleeting and subsides once the challenging situation passes. This is different from *being insecure* and experiencing a state of chronic low self-esteem in which anxiety is ever present and widespread. Interestingly, feelings of insecurity plague some of the most successful people in business, whom you would not expect to be hampered by insecurity.

- Howard Schultz, CEO of Starbucks, felt a great deal of insecurity as a kid. He grew up in federally subsidized housing; and his family lived on less than $20,000 a year, with no health insurance or worker's compensation when his father could not work. The kids were often maneuvering to avoid bill collectors. High levels of fear and uncertainty in childhood stunted the growth of his confidence. However, he overcame both his insecurity and his modest upbringing to successfully run a company with over 300,000 employees in more than 25,000 locations in 75 countries.[1]

- Oprah Winfrey grew up highly insecure as a result of childhood abuse and neglect. She was born on an isolated farm in rural Mississippi and her parents separated soon after she was born, leaving her in the care of her maternal grandmother. She suffered from serious abuse and was bounced from one caretaker to another. However, she was determined to work hard in school and developed the discipline to become an excellent student, ultimately going to Tennessee State University. She has since had her own television show, her own production company, and has become one of the wealthiest and most generous women in America.[2]

Howard Schultz and Oprah Winfrey are not alone in having experienced bouts of self-doubt and insecurity. In fact, many accomplished men and women at all levels of business have experienced anxiety, fear, and a serious lack of confidence at various times. No one escapes periodic self-questioning and lack of confidence. What differentiates healthy from unhealthy approaches to these insecurities is the degree to which they become debilitating and how effectively they are managed. Psychologists explain this difference by examining internal versus external *locus of control*. That is a fancy way of saying that the more we allow people and events to define us (external locus of control), the more likely we are to suffer serious bouts of self-doubt. In contrast, those who believe they can *choose* how they will respond to whatever they experience in life (internal locus of control) are more confident than those who feel powerless over external events.

People who are generally confident have a much greater sense of who they are, have a good sense of their strengths and weaknesses (and accept them), and believe that they will be able to be successful in most situations. They are planners more than worriers. However, the truth is that being human means we will all have times and situations in which we experience anxiety and feelings of insecurity.

A 2014 research study of 116 CEOs, both men and women, domestic and international, found executives have anxieties about:[3]

- Being seen as incompetent
- Underachieving
- Appearing too vulnerable
- Being politically attacked by colleagues
- Appearing foolish

These fears, all of which feed on insecurities, affect leaders' behaviors with their executive teams, lead to dysfunctional behaviors, and often result in poor decision-making. This poor decision-making results in focusing on survival rather than growth, inducing bad behavior at the next level down, and failing to act until there is a crisis. This is not to say that success is simply dependent on the degree of self-confidence a person has, nor does having a lack of confidence mean a person cannot rise in a company. Rather, it is how effectively individuals *manage* their insecurities that determines their ability to affect their outcomes. Such self-management can greatly impact an individual's success in an organization.

The Manifestation of Insecurity: Who Is Your Master

People who battle wavering self-confidence have several tendencies in common. Lack of self-confidence is typically expressed in one or more of the following patterns of thought, all of which have a history in an individual's psychological life. These patterns of thought are accompanied by symptoms of insecurity and behaviors that further feed insecurity.

Discounting Success

We regularly interview mid-career leaders who have risen quickly in their companies and have had a history of accomplishment. Our conversations inevitably lead to their aspirations and career desires and what it will take to achieve them. As they review their successes and begin mentally laying a foundation upon which to build future successes, they often hit a mental stumbling block. Have their successes really been due to their unique abilities, or just the good fortune of being in the right place at the right time? Most of these leaders are modest to the degree that they ascribe their accomplishments to external factors like having a good team, a good boss, or a particularly beneficial set of circumstances that allowed them to succeed. They have great difficulty taking credit for their success and owning their achievements. In fact, this syndrome has been given a name, the "imposter syndrome."[4] These leaders often confuse thinking less of themselves for being humble. However, as novelist C. S. Lewis observed, "humility is not thinking less of yourself, it is thinking of yourself less."[5]

In virtually all of these leaders, the same character flaw is present. Their view of themselves has not kept pace with the accomplishments they have achieved and the skills they have developed. They do, in fact, think less of themselves than their achievements warrant. Developmentally, the way we view ourselves is largely formed in the first ten years of our lives. At that time, psychological traits are created such as: the degree to which we have a sense of competence, willingness to take risks, comfort interacting with others, and ease in new and unfamiliar situations. People who have a lowered sense of self-esteem often carry around an arrested view of themselves. Though they are fully grown, they are stuck with the self-perception they had at ten years of age or younger. In psychologically healthy people, self-esteem and self-perception continues to adjust with subsequent experiences. The self-perception of healthy leaders keeps up with their growing mastery of life skills. In exploring the apprehensions of those individuals who do not feel confident in spite of numerous accomplishments, we have found time and again that their feelings about themselves are out-of-date. The good news is that, with work, this is a situation that can be corrected. Do not despair!

Using the Wrong Measuring Stick: Measuring Yourself Against Others

Judging your interior by others' exteriors is a losing proposition. This occurs when you use the *perceived* successes of others to measure your own *feelings* of success. There will always be someone wealthier, better looking, smarter, or more successful than you. The opposite is also true. There are infinite ways to feel less than, or more than, others. However, once you begin the process of comparing yourself to others, you begin scratching an itch for which there is no satisfaction.

Comparing ourselves to others is rooted in our desire to feel comfortable with where we are in life and silence our anxieties about not being good enough. We seek a metric by which to measure our happiness. I will be good enough when I achieve enough money, status, position, respect, and on and on. However, once we achieve those successes and milestones that we believed would indicate our success, we simply "move the goalposts" and push our measure of success farther away. We live in a competitive culture that encourages comparisons and is overly focused on winning. Taking a sideways glance is always a temptation for even healthy people. However, those with good self-esteem are able to put these comparisons in perspective and focus more on what is important to them, not what is important to their peer group or the rest of the world. They have an *internal* locus of control that serves them well.

The Propensity to Please: Looking for Love in All the Wrong Places

Insecurity often manifests in individuals as a desire to please others in order to feel good about themselves. Instead of seeking happiness through comparison with others, the propensity to please seeks happiness through the approval and acceptance of others. This pattern of thought can be witnessed in business when employees exchange the responsibility of how they feel about themselves for the approval of those with whom they work. They have a strong need to please their manager, their peers, and, even, subordinates. Their desire to please diminishes their ability to make independent decisions. As a result, they become dependent on the opinions of others. They live with a disproportionate amount of anxiety centered on avoiding the displeasure of others, instead of focusing on the quality or quantity of their work. They are fearful of doing or saying anything that may be controversial and they are most comfortable with repeating established routines. They have difficulty holding others accountable or having difficult conversations, for fear of being disliked.

This propensity to please is typically rooted in the relationship between individuals and their families-of-origin. Adult's feelings of worth are related to the degree to which they pleased their parents as children. Children can equate being loved with not displeasing the authority figures in their lives and they become adaptive and compliant to their parent's wishes. This fear of becoming a disappointment to others often generalizes beyond authority figures to others in some individuals' lives. Initially, their success in life may have been facilitated by their desire to please, but it reaches a ceiling when they are promoted to a management position in which they are required to make independent decisions and manage others by setting goals and holding them accountable. Pleasers struggle mightily to quell their anxieties about not being liked, which makes it difficult for them to take an unpopular or independent stand.

The Insecure Leader: Dominated by Anxiety

There is no way to completely avoid times and situations in which we feel anxious and insecure. It is not the absence of insecurity that defines confident leaders, but it is the recognition that they have insecurity and their ability to create plans to address those situations when they arise. Sigmund Freud recognized that humans are driven to reduce their feelings of anxiety. This is the human condition. Freud differentiated between objective anxiety, which is typical, and neurotic anxiety, which is excessive.[5] Objective anxiety arises from a threat from an external factor like a snarling dog or an impending accident. It is based in reality and the way to reduce anxiety in those situations is to remove oneself from them. On the other hand, neurotic anxiety is an internal conflict that is the fear of something happening for which there is little or no data to support that it might. An extreme example of this would be having anxiety over the belief you will be attacked by a bear when you are in the comfort of your apartment in lower Manhattan. It is this kind of neurotic anxiety that has taken residence in people who are chronically insecure. In our work with thousands of leaders, we have discovered that those leaders who are most insecure have usually adopted unhealthy and maladaptive behaviors to compensate. These leaders tend to fall into one of four categories.

Narcissistic Leaders

Narcissistic leaders compensate for their insecurities by having a grandiose sense of self-importance. Such leaders are the most profoundly insecure. They believe they are "special" and need excessive admiration from their subordinates, peers, and managers. They have a sense of entitlement and a strong belief in the "rightness" of their positions. They are preoccupied with power and authority. They exploit others, treating them in demeaning and patronizing ways. They are unwilling to admit to any wrongdoing and are highly defensive and or intimidating when challenged. The only employees who remain with a narcissistic manager are those who are highly dependent and lack esteem themselves.

Figure 8.1 Fear of failure

Source: andrewgenn.Depositphotos.com. http://depositphotos.com/63275605/stock-illustration-do-not-fail.html (accessed March 2017).

Narcissistic leaders have little difficulty setting a vision, but the visions they set are more a sense of their grandiosity than what is best for the business. Narcissistic leaders are the least likely to change because of their belief that any problems are the fault of others, and never their fault. When terminated, they are always certain they have been misunderstood and mistreated.

Avoidant Leaders

Avoidant leaders manage their anxiety by eluding interpersonal contact, especially in the midst of stressful situations. They are preoccupied with being judged or criticized, and find it easier to withdraw than deal with potential conflict. They are usually unwilling to take risks and have difficulty with interpersonal relationships because of deep-seated feelings of inadequacy. These leaders have difficulty communicating or delegating and they are passive managers. A chief information officer with whom we worked would often "disappear" in the midst of a big software conversion. On one occasion, she was found to be at home playing her piano while her subordinates were hard at work on one of these massive conversions.

Dependent Leaders

Dependent leaders manage their anxieties and insecurities by seeking excessive amounts of guidance and counsel on even routine decisions. They have difficulty doing things on their own or initiating new projects. Like the avoidant leader, they avoid conflict at all costs. They also have difficulty setting a vision, delegating, and holding people accountable. A branch manager of a bank with whom we consult is well liked but not respected by her employees. She had become so dependent on her manager's approval that she was wishy-washy on nearly all matters, frustrating her employees who were hungry for direction and decisiveness.

Obsessive Leaders

Obsessive leaders manage their fear by paying excessive attention to detail and checking and rechecking their work and the work of others. As with all types of anxious leaders, they have a high level of fear of scrutiny and an exaggerated sense of the consequences of others finding their work to be less than perfect. They can be preoccupied with rules and orderliness, at the expense of flexibility and efficiency. They can either have difficulty delegating or they micromanage others when they do delegate. There are clearly jobs where this kind of behavior is warranted and leads to success, such as software development, piloting an airplane, or some fields of medicine. In one hospital where we worked, the orthopedic surgeons were all prone to this kind of behavior. The checking, rechecking, and extensive oversight were the behaviors for which they were known. The operating room staff was always miserable but their patients were happy!

The aforementioned behaviors can appear to a lesser degree in all leaders. Sometimes leaders are overly bold when setting a vision or goal. At times, leaders want second opinions before taking action even after they, or their teams, have arrived at a conclusion. There are times when work is of such a sensitive and complex nature that it does require checking and double-checking. There are times when leaders need space to think things through away from the noise of the office. It is when a leader demonstrates a rigid, repetitive pattern of behavior, over time, that they have allowed their stress and anxieties to dominate their management and render it dysfunctional.

Healthy Leaders

Self-confident leaders are characterized by their ability to put anxiety and stress in context and "put their worry to work." These leaders evaluate themselves from the inside-out and not, like our insecure leaders, from the outside-in. They do not overestimate their weaknesses nor underestimate their strengths. They have allowed their history of success to strengthen their self-confidence, rather than seeing their successes as fleeting and accidental. They have times when they feel stressed, even intimidated, by challenging circumstances or people; but they create plans to deal with these difficult times rather than being paralyzed by the potential for failure. They spend more time planning to achieve results than worrying about what others may think. They judge themselves by their own internal set of standards, rather than how others may evaluate them.

We have explored the manifestations of insecurities in leaders. The question now remains: How do you increase your self-confidence so that you become the master of your work and personal life and learn to minimize the pressure of external situations or people?

The Esteem Machine: Developing a Stable Self-Confidence

Self-confident leaders have a different way of thinking about themselves and their achievements. Having such self-confidence means rethinking how you judge both successes and disappointments. You are not only as good as your last victory nor as bad as your last defeat. It is important to exit the roller coaster of valuing yourself solely based on successes and failures. People who never fail are never taking chances. It is more important to learn from failures than to wallow in disappointment of them, which is a form of dark narcissism. As business guru Tom Peters used to admonish, fail forward faster.

Cataloging Successes

When taking the sideways glance of comparison, there will always be people better and worse than you on any given dimension! Such comparisons are fruitless and discount the greatest value any person brings to a situation: his or her uniqueness. Capitalizing on this uniqueness is what leaders do best. When you think about your life thus far, what are the things you have accomplished? It is important to neither evaluate nor judge your accomplishments, just list them. These could be in the following areas found in Figure 8.2.

- **Relationships**: include friends, family, and so on.
- **Education**: include formal school and informal learning
- **Career**: include all jobs that you have had and your contributions
- **Personal**: what has contributed to who you are (such as participation in sports, arts, clubs, special interests, values)

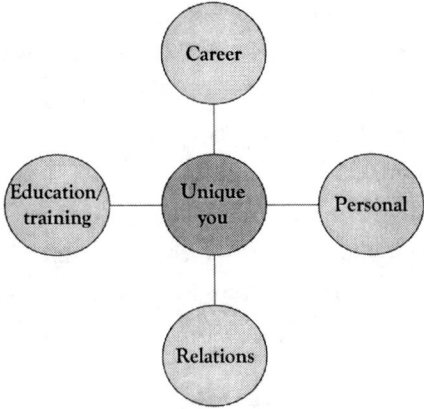

Figure 8.2 The confidence constellation

The goal of cataloging your distinctly personal experiences and accomplishments is to increasingly recognize the successes and achievements that have made you the unique person that you are. *The real challenge is to claim these!* When you reflect on the fact that you began life with a blank slate, what you have achieved is considerable. This exercise is a valuable tool to use in consolidating your gains and reinforcing your self-confidence. You have already achieved wonderful things, overcome many obstacles, and have the wherewithal to do more in the future.

Focusing on the Present

Contrary to popular belief, the mind can only focus on one thing at a time.[7] Being in the moment is central to achieving focus. The hallmark of confident people is the ability to apply laser focus to problem-solving, in the midst of both routine work and unforeseen challenges. Anxiety only comes when we are distracted by what we have done in the past or what the future may hold. Anxiety experienced in the present moment only occurs in the face of looming danger, which is very rare! The ability to immerse yourself in solving a challenging problem ensures that the problem will get the best of your attention. It is only in these moments when we experience calm emotions and freedom from attachment to results that we can be fully engaged in the process. Psychologists call this experience "flow," when your mind is fully immersed with a sense of energized focus and you lose all sense of time.[9] To achieve this flow it is essential to push away anxieties based in the past or future. Although the thoughts will likely occur, let them float away.

This present-moment focus will both alleviate insecurities that arise from anxiety and lead to a greater sense of competence. Self-confidence is closely tied to developing a conscious sense of competence or the awareness that you have the ability to solve difficult and challenging problems for which you have been trained.

Healthy Thinking → Healthy Behavior

One foundational process to undertake in the development of greater self-confidence is to manage how you interpret events and situations. The way we behave is dependent on how we feel, and how we feel is dependent on what we think. The process is as follows:[8]

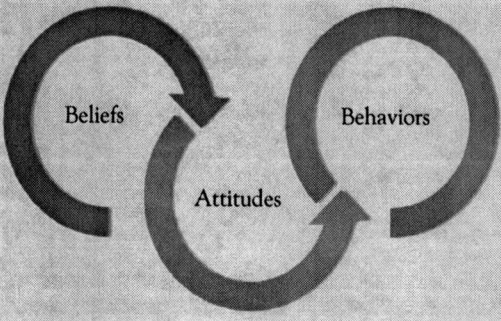

At their best, people with a healthy sense of self-esteem assess situations realistically and calmly manage their feelings. This process results in behaviors and actions that are appropriate for their situation. When those who have not learned to manage their insecurities enter into similar situations, they are likely to misinterpret events, which leads to feelings that are out of proportion and behaviors that are either under- or overreactions to the situation.

Oftentimes, employees are unexpectedly requested to meet with their manager. In this situation, a person with healthy self-esteem is surprised and curious (thoughts) with mild apprehension (feelings) and walks into the manager's office with an open mind and genuine interest in what the manager may say. The healthy individual is confident and comfortable.

In the same situation, an insecure person has exaggerated thoughts: "Am I in trouble? Will I get criticized? What have I done?" These thoughts lead to heightened feelings (despair, anxiety, shortness of breath). In such a state, an individual is likely to enter the manager's office exhibiting behaviors that are excessive (manic, restless, or withdrawn) and generally inappropriate for the situation. The manager may simply want to know the address of that great seafood restaurant where the team ate last week!

This is a simple example to demonstrate the typical levels of anxiety that plague an insecure person. However, there is a fix. It may not be possible to stop the thought, healthy or exaggerated, that comes into your mind as you assess a situation. These thoughts inevitably lead to feelings. However, before acting on your initial feelings, you can reassess the situation to determine if your thoughts were rational or a fearful product of your insecurity. That process looks like this:

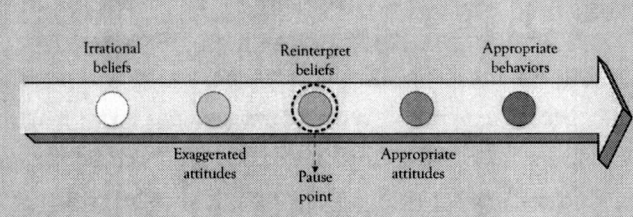

There is a *pause point* between feelings of anxiety and taking action, at which time it is important to determine if your thoughts are, in fact, rational and appropriate for the situation. Once this process becomes routine, the insecure person increasingly recognizes his or her patterns of irrational thinking. The individual can learn that the exaggerated thoughts and feelings he or she has are usually out of proportion to the situations he or she is in. With practice, thoughts become more tempered and inappropriate reactions and excessive feelings of anxiety begin to subside. Managing behavior is one of the greatest assets an individual can possess. This tool generalizes to virtually any situation and is particularly important for those in leadership positions.

Making Positive Allies

Confident leaders intentionally seek the company of other confident leaders. They are selective in choosing friends and associates. Author John Kuebler observed, "Show me your friends and I'll show you your future."[10] There is a concept that misery loves company. Those with low self-esteem tend to choose the company of others with low self-esteem. When people change, it is often those with whom they are closest who either resist their changing or, even, become obstacles to their change. It can be threatening to see someone with whom you are familiar transform into a healthier self-confident person. In order for individuals to have the best chance of making changes, they need to be supported by people who cheer them on and encourage them.

When asked to spend time with people in their organizations who seek their advice, we have observed that leaders are usually flattered and willing to give their time. It is increasingly common in organizations for formal and informal mentoring to take place. To supercharge your relationships, identify those in your organization whom you respect and believe would be able to help you in your development. Always have some objectives you want to achieve, have an agenda for a brief meeting, set a formal appointment with a potential mentor, and go for it! If the first leader turns you down, go down your list until you find someone who is willing to work with you. You will find your self-confidence soaring when you are able to engage in these relationships. Remember, it is always a good practice to "give to get." What can you offer the mentoring leader, so you will not just be a taker? Now what are you waiting for?

Having Commanding Conversations

Having powerful conversations begins with paying attention to the *kind* of conversations you have with yourself and others. The more we have conversations that are positive, hopeful, and free of complaining, the more we reinforce our ability to see possibilities rather than obstacles. On the other hand, having negative, complaint-filled conversations create an atmosphere of helplessness and victimization. It is not that one should disregard the realities of challenges. It is that confident people look for ways to solve difficult problems, rather than dwell on reasons they will not succeed. In your conversations with yourself and others, you want to move from victim to victor. This positive framing of conversations will automatically lead to a boost in your self-esteem.

The *content* of your conversations also determines the level of potency of the discussion. As Eleanor Roosevelt observed, "Great minds discuss ideas; average minds discuss events; small minds discuss people."[11] Leaders who have powerful conversations are regularly talking about ideas for their organization, new ways to innovate, process or product improvements, and so on. This implies that they are learners and always curious about how to improve themselves and their business. In other words, in order to be a good conversationalist, you need to have something compelling to say! Being a lifelong learner is central to having interesting and provocative conversations. An added bonus is that talking about things that matter to you generates self-confidence. Never miss an opportunity to let your ideas be heard, respectfully and confidently.

Creating an Impressive Presence

In today's "business-casual" work environment, people are encouraged to wear clothes to work that make them feel comfortable. While comfort at work is a worthy goal, avoid getting lulled into the trap of dressing lazily or sloppily. The way we dress affects the way we feel and the way we view ourselves. If we wear pajamas, we will likely want to sit on the couch and watch Netflix. If we wear a tuxedo or ball gown, we will want to go to a formal affair. Wearing clothes that make you feel professional and attractive increases your confidence.

Accepting Yourself

An often-overlooked aspect of self-esteem involves coming to terms with your own limits. Just as we all have our unique strengths and talents, we are also all flawed and fall short in some areas. Operating on the basis that one should be competent or perfect at everything is a recipe for life-long misery. Self-acceptance of both our gifts *and* our limitations leads to authentic competence and peace of mind. Being able to accept credit for your successes and openly owning your failures, as well as what you learned from them, will evoke the admiration and respect of others.

Change comes in fits and starts. Sometimes the changes we make are easy and require little effort. However, increasing self-confidence is not easy work and not for the weak-willed. This work requires courage, persistence, and the ability to treat yourself kindly when you slip up. Most of all, it requires a plan and tools. We can say unequivocally that the success you experience in life is closely tied to your self-confidence. In this chapter, we have provided several tools and resources. Now, it is up to you to create a plan!

Coach's Corner

Bouts of insecurity plague everyone. The anxiety that stems from insecurity is not, in and of itself, a detriment to success or happiness. It is the ways in which we choose to *react* to our insecurities that defines us. The most successful leaders have learned how to control their insecurities, rather than letting their insecurities control them. The good news is that self-confidence is a practice that can be learned.

Three Tips for Cultivating Self-Confidence

1. **Find your "Pause Point"**
   - When you find yourself reacting negatively to a situation, take a moment to pause and reassess. Are your emotions in line with the reality of the situation? If not, allow yourself to reinterpret the situation and act from a place of control rather than gut reaction.
2. **Avoid mental traps**
   - Negative patterns of thought that lead to low self-esteem are ubiquitous. They include undervaluing yourself, comparing yourself to others, and letting the feelings and

Chapter 8 Survey

Effective delegation	Much too little		Barely too little		Just right	Barely too much		Much too much	
	−4	−3	−2	−1	0	+1	+2	+3	+4
Please insert an "X" in the appropriate box to indicate your answer									
How often do you take a "pause point" when you experience a spike in negative emotions?									
How often do you value yourself based on the opinions of others?									
How often do you find yourself comparing your life to the lives' of others?									

opinions of others influence the way you value yourself. Such negative patterns of thought only serve to increase insecurities.

3. **Practice self-acceptance**
   - Everyone experiences bouts of insecurity and everyone fails. Do not judge yourself too harshly. Own your shortcomings and learn from your failures so that they become building blocks for your future successes.

Areas for Development

What are the top three steps you could take to improve your self-confidence?

1. _____

2. _____

3. _____

Notes

1. Clifford (2016).
2. Jones (2015).
3. Brooks (1999).
4. Clance and Imes (1978).
5. Deseret News Faith (2012).
6. Abel (2017).
7. Ballard (2017).
8. Beck (2011).
9. Csikszentmihalyi (1990).
10. Kepcher (2011).
11. Roosevelt (2017).

References

Abel, S, Dr. 2017. *Types of Anxiety, Personality Psychology*, February 19. http://doctorabel.us/personality-psychology/types-of-anxiety.html (accessed March 1, 2017).

Ballard, W. 2017. "The Fallacy of Multitasking." *Entrepreneur,* January 20. https://entrepreneur.com/article/286794 (accessed March 1, 2017).

Beck, J.S. 2011. *Cognitive behavior therapy: Basics and beyond.* 2nd ed. New York: The Guilford Press.

Brooks, P. 1999. *Oprah Winfrey: A Voice for the People.* New York: Franklin Watts.

Clance, P.R., and S. Imes. 1978. "The Imposter Phenomenon in High Achieving Women: Dynamics and Therapeutic Intervention." *Psychotherapy: Theory, Research and Practice* 15, no. 3, pp. 241–47.

Clifford, C. 2016. "How Starbucks' Howard Schultz went from the Projects to Creating 300,000 Jobs and a $3 Billion Fortune." *CNBC,* December 2. http://cnbc.com/2016/12/02/how-starbucks-howard-schultz-went-from-the-projects-to-creating-300000-jobs-and-a-3-billion-fortune.html (accessed March 1, 2017).

Csikszentmihalyi, M. 1990. *Flow: The Psychology of Optimal Experience.* New York: Harper & Row.

Deseret News Faith Retrieved from June 27, 2012. *http://deseretnews.com/top/817/0/Top-100-CS-Lewis-quotes-.html*

Jones, R. 2015. "What are CEOs Afraid of," *Harvard Business Review Leadership,* February 24. https://hbr.org/2015/02/what-ceos-are-afraid-of.html (accessed March 1, 2017).

Kepcher, C. 2011. "The People You Surround Yourself With Can Help (or Hurt) Your Career, So Choose Wisely." *New York Daily News,* April 1. www.nydailynews.com/.../people-surround-hurt-career-choose-wisely-article.html (accessed March 1, 2017).

Roosevelt, E. 2017. Great Minds Discuss Ideas; Average Minds Discuss Events; Small Minds Discuss People. https://brainyquote.com/quotes/quotes/e/eleanorroo385439.html (accessed March 2017).

CHAPTER 9

Designing Your Future

When a good leadership conference ends or you finish reading a good book, you end up buzzing with energy and full of inspiration. But conference notes usually get stuffed into a folder and wind up in the back of a filing cabinet. Books usually wind up on a dusty shelf, never to be seen again. Even when we learn something that feels inspiring, our behavior is rarely changed. The purpose of reading a book on leadership, going to a conference or workshop, or getting an additional degree is to fundamentally change the way you think about a topic and, ultimately, change your behavior. However, without reinforcement of the learning and a *plan* for making changes, the new knowledge you may have gained becomes lost. Research conducted by Hermann Ebbinghaus over a century ago, and replicated numerous times since, concluded that a startling amount of information is quickly forgotten for lack of reinforcement.[1] Humans tend to recall only half of their newly learned knowledge in a matter of days or weeks, unless consciously reviewed (see Figure 9.1). Just trying

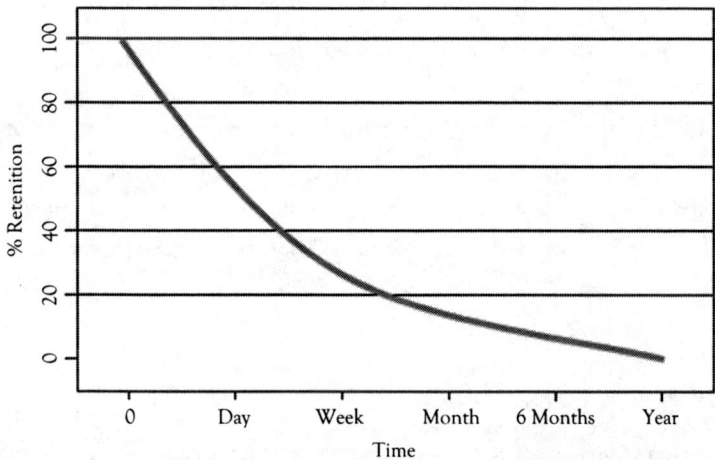

Figure 9.1 Forgetting curve

to remember important nuggets of learning is difficult, even after a short time. You may remember the feeling of being inspired by groundbreaking information, but that feeling is not sufficient in and of itself.

The question remains, how can the information from this book be translated into new behavior that will make a difference in the lives of readers? In this chapter, we provide you with the tools to turn your goals into realities.

The Importance of Setting Goals

It has been determined that the likelihood of accomplishing a goal increases exponentially if the goal is stated. In fact, research by Dr. Gail Matthews at the Dominican University at California determined the following relationship between one's management of goals and the likelihood of accomplishing them:[2]

- A goal is more likely to be accomplished if it is stated.
- A goal is significantly more likely to be accomplished if it is written down.
- Making a *public commitment* to achieving a goal makes its accomplishment significantly more likely than just saying or writing it down.
- Being *accountable* to others for achieving a goal makes its accomplishment significantly more likely than the use of the previous strategies without including accountability.

Dr. Matthew's research determined that that there are three keys to actually accomplishing goals: *writing down goals, commitment, and accountability*. It makes sense that when you make the effort to specify a goal, commit to the goal, and enlist assistance, your likelihood of accomplishing it increases. Do not wait to get started!

Determining Your Goals

In **Coach's Corner** at the end of each chapter, you identified three growth areas that will help you become a more effective leader. The range of these growth areas should be broad and include both personal and professional aspects.

List the goals you have identified from the end of each chapter:

Chapter	Goals
Chapter 1	1.
	2.
	3.
Chapter 2	1.
	2.
	3.
Chapter 3	1.
	2.
	3.
Chapter 4	1.
	2.
	3.
Chapter 5	1.
	2.
	3.
Chapter 6	1.
	2.
	3.
Chapter 7	1.
	2.
	3.
Chapter 8	1.
	2.
	3.

The goals you have identified are all worthy of your consideration and may all be important in career growth and development. However, increasing the likelihood of successful behavioral change requires further sharpening your focus by prioritizing no more than three goals at a time. As discussed in Chapter 3, the key to accomplishing goals is to focus on only a few and make sure they are critical to your overall success.[3] Now that you have compiled your goals, we want you to identify the three that are most important for you to undertake now. Keep in mind that you need to choose those changes that will make the greatest difference to you, your team, and your company. Use the tips in each of the chapters, as well as those in Coach's Corner, to assist you in creating your goals. From the aforementioned list, now select the three goals that you would most like to pursue.

Top Three Goals

1. _____

2. _____

3. _____

Translating Your Goals Into a Plan

The difference between a wish and a goal is the development of a plan. A wish without a plan is mere fantasy. Now that you have identified your top three goals, you can use the following template to create a plan to ensure that you will follow through. Make sure the goals meet the SMART criteria for writing a good goal:

- **Specific**: The more specific you are, the easier it will be to identify and maintain your target. For example, do not say you want to lose weight. Specify the exact number of pounds you want to lose.
- **Measurable**: It is critical to have a way to quantify your goal so that you know when you have achieved it.
- **Achievable**: Create goals that are possible to accomplish, neither too easy nor too difficult. Goals that are either too low or too high are less likely to be accomplished than goals that are achievable even if they are a stretch.
- **Relevant**: Create goals that will actually contribute to your success as a leader.

- **Time Bound**: Having deadlines to accomplish all, or part, of the goal are important. Create a time frame that is reasonable, not too soon nor too far out.

Use this template to create your Personal Goal Plan:

Personal Goal Plan

Identify the goal	*Describe what you want to be different and how it will help you be a more effective leader.*
State current situation	*What are you currently doing that prohibits you from being as effective as you would like to be?*
Identify the objective	*In a single statement, describe what success would look like if you were to accomplish the goal.*
Create a plan	*Use the SMART sequence here to bring the goal to life:* *Specific:* *Measurable:* *Attainable:* *Relevant:* *Time-Bound:*
Overcome obstacles	*Identify the obstacles you anticipate in the accomplishing of the goal and the strategies you have to overcome them. Examples include irrational thinking; people enabling unwanted behaviors; emotional triggers; and so on.*
Recruit support	*Identify those with whom you can share your goal and how they will hold you accountable for making progress on the goal.*
Review improvement	*When you look at your timetable for accomplishing the goal, set up quarterly reviews to determine how you are doing, what revisions you may need to make and how you can consolidate your gains.*

Now create a plan for each of your three main goals, using the templates provided later. It may take a little time to formulate your thoughts into full-fledged plans for your goals, but it will be worth reaping the full rewards of the work you put in.

Designing Your Future: A Leader's Development

One of our clients identified an individual for the high potential program whose thinking about the business was very well developed but her management behavior needed some improvement. Her manager noted that she was a highly capable individual who worked long hours, almost excessively, and that her subordinates did not appear to be bearing as much of the load as they should. She determined from reading Chapter 4, about delegation, that her major deficit was her lack of assertiveness with her employees. Furthermore, she acknowledged that her propensity to please resulted in not requiring as much of her employees as she could because of her desire for them to like her. An inadvertent consequence was that she was completing the work of her subordinates that was too tactical for her position and not focusing enough on the strategic demands of her position. We discussed this with her and she came to the conclusion that there were times when she needed to take charge, delegate responsibilities more clearly, declare her position, and require more of her subordinates. We worked with her to develop a specific Personal Goal Plan to address this problem as follows.

Personal Goal Plan

Identify the goal	I want to leverage my leadership by delegating more work to my subordinates in an effective manner.
State current situation	Currently, I do not differentiate my workload sufficiently to determine the items on which I should work, those that I should disregard altogether, and those I should be delegating. This problem results in my working on items that others could manage as well taking up time I need for higher priorities.
Identify the objective	By delegating more effectively, I would be working on those responsibilities that are most important for my position, delegating those items appropriate for my subordinates, and increasing the overall productivity and impact of my organization.
	Use the SMART sequence here to bring the goal to life: **Specific**: Every morning I will look at the items on my agenda for the day and determine whether I should do them, delegate them, or discard them. I will delegate those items appropriate for my subordinates and set explicit timelines and expectations regarding the quality of their work. *Measurable*: On a weekly basis, I will keep a log of all remaining items, review the log to determine where I have succeeded in delegating and holding subordinates accountable, where I have failed and assess the causes for delegation or accountability failure. *Attainable*: I want to delegate all of the work that others can manage and allow my subordinates to tell me if they are overloaded, rather than deciding ahead of time what their load should be. I will use their feedback to determine subsequent delegation.

Create a plan	**Relevant**: As I review the items for which I have responsibility, I will become much more diligent in turning down items that are not appropriate for our department or for me personally. I will focus on results rather than on pleasing others. **Time-Bound**: At the end of each week, I will review the log I have created and determine how successful I have become in delegating. On a monthly basis, I will review the log with my manager and solicit her feedback.
Overcome obstacles	Most of the obstacles I need to overcome in order to accomplish this goal are self-imposed, including my penchant to please and my impatience in doing work myself rather than developing others and delegating. As I review my item log daily and weekly, I will determine the causes of poorly delegated work and focus on correcting the problems the following week.
Recruit support	Initially, I will tell my subordinates that I am determined to become a more effective delegator and that they should expect the responsibility for more work. Also, it will be up to them to let me know when they are overloaded with work. I will meet with my manager monthly to review my item log and continue to look for ways to improve and con-gratulate myself on successive accomplishments toward the goal.
Review improvement	I will review this goal with my manager to solicit her support. In addition, I will review the item log with her monthly and solicit her feedback for ways to build on my developing better delegation skills.

By using this Personal Goal Plan, our client has created a framework for becoming a more effective delegator. She has identified a number of areas for her growth and development, focused on the one area that would add the greatest value (delegation) and created a concrete plan to accomplish her goal. By letting both her staff and her manager know of her plan, her chances of accomplishing it are much greater than just keeping it to herself. By having specific times when she will review her goal with her manager, she is creating a pattern of accountability to further ensure her success in goal accomplishment. She is designing her future!

We have included blank Personal Goal Plans in our Appendix for you to create your own goal plans. It can be copied for creating additional plans.

Things to Keep in Mind

Once you have created a **Personal Goal Plan** for achieving the three goals you have identified, we encourage you to set a target completion date and get started! As you begin, keep in mind a few things that will help you stay on track. The execution of any plan requires the discipline to continue the process until either your goal is completed, a new and better goal emerges, or the goal is determined to be unworthy of pursuit. All three outcomes require perseverance to determine the best outcome. Make a commitment to yourself to persist.

Any goal worthy of attainment will be met with periodic setbacks, often the result of poor execution, inattention, or discouragement. At such times, it is important to remember that you are human, forgive yourself, and move forward. The more you dwell on a setback, the less likely you are to continue to pursue your goal. Cut yourself some slack and move forward.

On the other hand, when you experience small successes along the way to goal completion, it is important to reward yourself. Relax and

"Let's just say he's heightened his expectations."

Figure 9.2 High expectations

Source: andrewgenn/Depositphotos.com. http://depositphotos.com/16179317/stock-photo-lets-just-say-hes-heightened.html (accessed March 12, 2017).

enjoy the moment. You are going in the right direction and this is an indication that you are closer to the outcome you desire. Keep up the good work! Likewise, share your successes with others, small or large. Accountability does not only mean that you are doing that to which you committed, it also means that you are giving others a chance to validate your advancement.

Once you have accomplished the outcome of your goal, claim it! You have worked hard to change and it is time to be bold in acknowledging to yourself, and others, the remarkable accomplishment you have achieved! Congratulations on beginning the journey to being a more effective and capable leader! Moving from being a good leader to a great leader is a process with many unexpected twists and turns. The good news is that you are now in the driver's seat of your journey and taking the first steps to becoming a great leader. Who knows, this may be the first of many transformational changes on your journey as a leader!

We Would Like to Hear from You

You have elected to go on a journey that requires discipline, perseverance, and courage. Making changes is not easy and you have begun what many others only imagine. We would like to hear about your journey, your successes, frustrations, and, most of all, the outcomes of working through your plan. This will give you one additional form of accountability.

Coach's Corner

It is easy for leaders to get excited by new ideas and practices, but often difficult for them to translate these ideas into actions. Only by having a plan is it possible for a leader to transform a wish into a reality. Narrow down your goals, create measurable plans, and follow through!

Three Tips for Creating Your Plan

1. **Announce your goals**
   - Simply sharing your goals with others will give you a level of accountability that can take you one step closer to accomplishing them. If someone you trust can hold you accountable, that is even better.
2. **Create SMART goals**
   - It is easy for goals to become so abstract that they are impossible to accomplish. Keep your goals as concrete as possible for best results. Make sure they are: **specific, measurable, attainable, relevant, and time-bound.**
3. **Pace yourself**
   - Achieving major goals requires patience and tenacity. It can take weeks, months, and even years. Celebrate your successes along the way, and do not sweat the small stuff. Failures are inevitable stepping stones on the road to success.

Areas for Development

What are the top three goals you would like to take from this book? Create your plans and execute them!

1. _____

2. _____

3. _____

Notes

1. Ebbinghaus (1913).
2. Matthews (2015).
3. McChesney, Covey, and Huling (2012).

References

Ebbinghaus, H. 1913. *Memory: A Contribution to Experimental Psychology.* New York City Teacher College, Columbia University.

Matthews, G, Dr. 2015. "Study Focuses on Strategies for Achieving Goals, Resolutions." paper presented at the ninth annual International Conference of the Psychology Research Unit of Athens Institute for Education and Research (ATINER), May.

McChesney, C., S. Covey and J. Huling. 2012. *The 4 Disciplines of Execution.* New York: Simon & Schuster.

Appendixes

Personal Goal Plan

Name: **Goal #1**

Identify the goal	
State current situation	
Identify the objective	
Create a plan	*Use the SMART sequence here to bring the goal to life:* *Specific:* *Measurable:* *Attainable:* *Relevant:* *Time-Bound:*
Overcome obstacles	
Recruit support	
Review improvement	

Personal Goal Plan

Name: **Goal #2**

Identify the goal	
State current situation	
Identify the objective	
Create a plan	*Use the SMART sequence here to bring the goal to life:* *Specific:* *Measurable:* *Attainable:* *Relevant:* *Time-Bound:*
Overcome obstacles	
Recruit support	
Review improvement	

Personal Goal Plan

Name: **Goal #3**

Identify the goal	
State current situation	
Identify the objective	
Create a plan	*Use the SMART sequence here to bring the goal to life:* *Specific:* *Measurable:* *Attainable:* *Relevant:* *Time-Bound:*
Overcome obstacles	
Recruit support	
Review improvement	

About the Authors

Myron J. Beard, PhD, is a business psychologist and world-class consultant, coach, and speaker. He is founder and principal of Beard Executive Consulting, a company that consults executives on strategy development, aligning structure to strategy, and executive and team development. Since starting his company in 2006, he has worked extensively with executives across industries assisting leaders and organizations to enhance their personal and business performance. His PhD is in Counseling Psychology.

Based in Denver, Colorado, he has worked with clients around the world. Clients range from small privately held companies to large multinational companies. Companies with whom he has worked include: First Data Corporation (worldwide), Western Union Corporation (worldwide), Harnischfeger Corporation, Hill's Pet Products, Joy Mining Manufacturing (United States, UK, Australia, South Africa), Dobson Park (UK), Longwall Corporation (Australia), KN Energy, The Industrial Company (TIC), Kiewit, Kansas State University College of Veterinary Medicine, Kaiser Permanente (CO), Colorado Children's Hospital, Nebraska Public Power District, Orica Mining Services (United States, Europe, Australia, Singapore, South America) Presbyterian Health Plan (NM), Xcel Energy, Public Service of NM, Montana Power Company, Cupertino Electric, Ball Aerospace, Best Western, Dial Corporation, Anthem Blue Cross/ Blue Shield, TeleCheck, GE Johnson Construction, Carondelet Health System, Rio Rancho School District, and numerous other organizations.

During the course of his career, he has worked with thousands of executives facilitating strategy development, helping create high-performing teams in extreme work environments, leading international merger integration efforts, and working with companies to assist them in their restructuring efforts. He has interviewed and assessed hundreds of executives for development, promotion, and hiring decisions. It has been as a result of these numerous evaluations that the idea for *The DNA of Leadership* was developed. He has also authored numerous articles and book chapters. In 2007, Myron coauthored *Merger Integration: a CEOs field guide to the art & process of effective merger integration.* This book has been used as a guide in numerous merger integration projects internationally.

In addition to his consulting work, he has served on numerous non-profit boards, including the Western Union Foundation, ArtReach (Chairman), Denver Chamber of Commerce (Healthcare Committee), Gold Crown Foundation, Littleton ISD Gifted and Talented Committee, Daniels College of Business Advisory Board, Iliff Seminary Advisory Board, Smeal Graduate School of Business Advisory Board, and has served as an Executive Fellow and founding mentor at Daniels College of Business. In addition, Myron and his wife, Ann, serve as senior advisors to, and mentors in, the Denver Tech Center Chamber of Commerce *Young Professional's Mentoring Program.*

Myron and Ann have four children in four different states and two grandchildren. He likes to travel and has been to 49 of the 50 states (lacking West Virginia); six of seven continents (lacking Antarctica) and nearly 40 countries. They reside in Greenwood Village, Colorado.

E-mail: MyronBeard@BeardExecutiveConsulting.com

Alan Weiss, PhD, is one of those rare people who can say he is a consultant, speaker, and author and mean it. His consulting firm, Summit Consulting Group, Inc., has attracted clients such as Merck, Hewlett-Packard, GE, Mercedes-Benz, State Street Corporation, Times Mirror Group, The Federal Reserve, The New York Times Corporation, Toyota, and over 500 other leading organizations. He has served on the boards of directors of the Trinity Repertory Company, a Tony-Award-winning New England regional theater, Festival Ballet, and chaired the Newport International Film Festival.

His speaking typically includes 20 keynotes a year at major conferences, and he has been a visiting faculty member at Case Western Reserve University, Boston College, Tufts, St. John's, the University of Illinois, the Institute of Management Studies, and the University of Georgia Graduate School of Business. He has held an appointment as adjunct professor in the Graduate School of Business at the University of Rhode Island where he taught courses on advanced management and consulting skills. He once held the record for selling out the highest priced workshop (on entrepreneurialism) in the then-21-year history of New York City's

Learning Annex. His PhD is in psychology. He has served on the Board of Governors of Harvard University's Center for Mental Health and the Media.

He is an inductee into the Professional Speaking Hall of Fame® and the concurrent recipient of the National Speakers Association Council of Peers Award of Excellence, representing the top 1% of professional speakers in the world. He has been named a Fellow of the Institute of Management Consultants, one of only two people in history holding both those designations.

His prolific publishing includes over 500 articles and 60 books, including his best-seller, *Million Dollar Consulting* (from McGraw-Hill). His newest is *Lifestorming* (with Marshall Goldsmith, Wiley). His books have been on the curricula at Villanova, Temple University, and the Wharton School of Business, and have been translated into 12 languages.

He is interviewed and quoted frequently in the media. His career has taken him to 60 countries and 49 states. (He is afraid to go to North Dakota.) *Success Magazine* cited him in an editorial devoted to his work as "a worldwide expert in executive education." The *New York Post* called him "one of the most highly regarded independent consultants in America." He is the winner of the prestigious Axiem Award for Excellence in Audio Presentation.

He is the recipient of the Lifetime Achievement Award of the American Press Institute, the first-ever for a non-journalist, and one of only seven awarded in the 65-year history of the association. He holds an annual Thought Leadership Conference which draws world famous experts as speakers. In 2016 his featured speaker is Harvard Distinguished Professor Dan Gilbert, whose work on happiness has drawn over 15 million TED views.

He has coached the former and present Miss Rhode Island/Miss America candidates in interviewing skills. He once appeared on the popular American TV game show *Jeopardy*, where he lost badly in the first round to a dancing waiter from Iowa.

Alan is married to the lovely Maria for 49 years, and they have two children and twin granddaughters. They reside in East Greenwich, RI with their dogs, Buddy Beagle and Bentley, a white German Shepherd.

Index

OTHER TITLES IN THE HUMAN RESOURCE MANAGEMENT AND ORGANIZATIONAL BEHAVIOR COLLECTION

- *The Illusion of Inclusion: Global Inclusion, Unconscious Bias, and the Bottom Line* by Helen Turnbull
- *On All Cylinders: The Entrepreneur's Handbook* by Ron Robinson
- *Employee LEAPS: Leveraging Engagement by Applying Positive Strategies* by Kevin E. Phillips
- *Making Human Resource Technology Decisions: A Strategic Perspective* by Janet H. Marler and Sandra L. Fisher
- *Feet to the Fire: How to Exemplify And Create The Accountability That Creates Great Companies* By Lorraine A. Moore
- *HR Analytics and Innovations in Workforce Planning* By Tony Miller
- *Deconstructing Management Maxims, Volume I: A Critical Examination of Conventional Business Wisdom* by Kevin Wayne
- *Deconstructing Management Maxims, Volume II: A Critical Examination of Conventional Business Wisdom* by Kevin Wayne
- *The Real Me: Find and Express Your Authentic Self* by Mark Eyre
- *Across the Spectrum: What Color Are You?* by Stephen Elkins-Jarrett
- *The Human Resource Professional's Guide to Change Management: Practical Tools and Techniques to Enact Meaningful and Lasting Organizational Change* by Melanie J. Peacock
- *Tough Calls: How to Move Beyond Indecision and Good Intentions* by Linda D. Henman

Announcing the Business Expert Press Digital Library

Concise e-books business students need for classroom and research

This book can also be purchased in an e-book collection by your library as

- a one-time purchase,
- that is owned forever,
- allows for simultaneous readers,
- has no restrictions on printing, and
- can be downloaded as PDFs from within the library community.

Our digital library collections are a great solution to beat the rising cost of textbooks. E-books can be loaded into their course management systems or onto students' e-book readers.
The **Business Expert Press** digital libraries are very affordable, with no obligation to buy in future years. For more information, please visit **www.businessexpertpress.com/librarians**. To set up a trial in the United States, please email **sales@businessexpertpress.com**.

CPSIA information can be obtained
at www.ICGtesting.com
Printed in the USA
FSOW01n1842220118
43470FS